PRAISE FOR

SELF AS COACH, SELF AS LEADER

With our profession entering its next stage of maturity, coaches must do the same. Written by one of the legends of the field, McLean lays out a compelling roadmap to help coaches go from good to great. This book will push you, challenge you, grow you. Don't read it lightly!

—**Brian O. Underhill**, PhD, Founder and CEO, CoachSource, LLC

Pam McLean has created a master class on how to become a great coach by mining the depths of one's self and full potential. A perfect blend of art and science combined with her own unique wisdom and personal insights, honed by over 35 years of practice; the one definitive book on coaching for all current and aspiring coaches.

—**Steve Milovich**, Professor, Jon M. Huntsman School of Business Former SVP Human Resources, The Walt Disney Company

Pamela McLean has created a profoundly valuable coaching book for both new and experienced coaches. *Self as Coach, Self as Leader* teaches us the essence of how to develop ourselves into uniquely wise and effective coaches. She is one of the original master teachers of a rich, developmental style of coaching and her book is packed full of not only her own personal reflections on developing coaching excellence but also in-depth coaching vignettes that are superbly helpful to the reader. This book has my strongest recommendation.

—**Jeffrey E. Auerbach**, PhD, President of the College of Executive Coaching Coauthor of *Positive Psychology in Coaching*

The coaching field, and all the "interaction sciences" like mentoring and managing, needs this book. So much of what is practiced in these sciences is not rooted in the deeper knowledge and principles from which our practices stem. Read this book to learn why and how we need to do what works with clients of all types in an endless number of situations. Pam McLean is a gift to the field, with a gift of elegant depth and doable practices.

—**John Schuster**, Executive Coach, Facilitator at Columbia University's Coach Certification Program
Author of *Answering Your Call* and *The Power of Your Past*

Drawing on her extensive experience as therapist, coach, and leader, Pam McLean, co-founder and CEO of the Hudson Institute of Coaching, adds new dimensions to the profession of coach. Interweaving personal examples with samples of client coach interactions, and adding practices to carry the work forward, McLean demonstrates the what, the why, and the how of the elusive concept of bringing one's own self to the encounter with the client in service to the client's needs.

—**Patricia Adson**, PhD, Master Coach, author of *Depth Coaching*

McLean once again brings the heat! To serve high-performing leaders, coaches must first serve themselves: a process of self-leadership that requires deep inner work—way beyond what's comfortable—toward an evolved coaching character. For those with the courage to go, the roadmap is right here.

—**Ray Luther**, Senior Lecturer, Management & Entrepreneurship, Kelley School of Business, Indiana University

Pam McLean is a thought leader who embodies the knowledge and wisdom that she imparts in her book. Her willingness to share her own journey as a coach sets this book apart. You will not only gain a deeper understanding of the coaching profession and gain new insights from her model and framework, but you will come to admire her as a mentor, teacher, and guide.

—**Dr. Beverly Kaye**, Coauthor of *Love 'Em or Lose 'Em, Up Is Not the Only Way*, and *Help Them Grow or Watch Them Go, and* Founder, Career Systems International

Coaching is the inner game of change; it will transform self and leaders. This is the great guidebook to make transformation happen.

—**David Dan**, Intel Former President, Taiwan/China/Hong Kong, Hong Kong University SPACE program executive coach faculty

As a leader or coach, do you keep that remarkable instrument, your "self," as fit as you keep your body? If it hasn't occurred to you, then try this remarkable, honest, practical book. It makes difficult theory clear and useful, and brings in new material that might surprise even the world's best coaches. The greater the challenges, the more you need yourself to be better tuned.

—**Anne Scoular**, Cofounder, Meyler Campbell, and Visiting Scholar at Oxford Saïd Business School

Awareness precedes choice! When we are able to truly understand our inner landscape and be awake to the narratives and beliefs that run and live within us, we are able to make choices that have the potential to positively impact our lives and those around us.

—**Penny Handscomb**, Partner, Omidyar Network

The future of leadership is coaching! *Self as Coach, Self as Leader* supports leaders in knowing themselves. This self-knowledge is mandatory to navigate the increasingly complex business landscape.

—**Dawn Sharifan**, Head of People Operations, Slack Technology

The wisdom in *Self as Coach, Self as Leader* is exactly what the coaching profession needs to catapult its empowering impact on the leaders we need in this increasingly challenging world.

—**Marilee Adams**, PhD, Author of *Change Your Questions, Change Your Life*

This book is a seamless blend of Pam's personal and professional experiences and the best academic research in the field of leadership coaching. Pam masterfully partners with you and leads you on a fascinating journey of continuing self-discovery. Your clients will be very glad you read this book. They should read it, too.

—**Steve Knight**, Executive Coach and Adjunct Professor of Business Communication, INSEAD

An inspiring and electrifying read that compels the insightful coach to explore and embrace their deepest self to fully cultivate their craft. Vital for anyone coaching physicians grappling with redefining their identities when embarking on career role changes.

—**Elizabeth Brill**, MD, MBA, Chief Medical Officer

Once again, Pamela McLean provides a comprehensive and deeply resourced guide for developmental coaching in the twenty-first century—an awe-inspiring gift to all coaches. Through McLean's deep understanding of the demands on today's leaders to lead in "tumultuous and unpredictable times," she challenges and inspires her readers to broaden their knowledge and deepen the quality and capacity of their coaching through increased self-awareness as coaches and leaders.

—**Cathy Medeiros**, Global Vice President,
Inclusion and Diversity, Eaton

Self as Coach, Self as Leader is a shining star in a cosmos of somewhat shallow how-to books on leadership. Its deep insights go to the heart of what really matters to becoming an evolved coach, leader and person—transforming self.

—**Louise M. Morman**, Executive Director, Lockheed
Martin Leadership Institute, Miami University

Any leader or person who wants to build or grow leadership capacity would benefit from Pam's book. We face ever-increasing challenges in today's rapidly changing employment environment, and improving your inner game has become an essential mechanism to overcoming these challenges. *Self as Coach, Self as Leader* not only offers a powerful learning approach that is highly relevant to leaders, but also shares Pam's reflections on her journey as a track record coach and researcher. This book played a role in my personal leadership transformation journey, and I hope you enjoy it as much as I did.

—**Cici Li**, VP of Human Resource, Shanghai Disney Resort

Bombs of wisdom from the queen of coaching! It's like having Pam McLean in your back pocket.

—**Amy Hayes**, V.P. Facebook Global Learning and Development

self

AS

COACH

**DEVELOPING THE BEST IN YOU
TO DEVELOP THE BEST IN OTHERS**

self

AS

LEADER

PAMELA MᶜLEAN

WILEY

Published by John Wiley & Sons, Inc., Hoboken, New Jersey.
Published simultaneously in Canada.

For general information on our other products and services or for technical support, please contact our Customer Care Department within the United States at (800) 762-2974, outside the United States at (317) 572-3993 or fax (317) 572-4002.

Wiley publishes in a variety of print and electronic formats and by print-on-demand. Some material included with standard print versions of this book may not be included in e-books or in print-on-demand. If this book refers to media such as a CD or DVD that is not included in the version you purchased, you may download this material at http://booksupport.wiley.com. For more information about Wiley products, visit www.wiley.com.

Library of Congress Cataloging-in-Publication Data:

Names: McLean, Pamela D., author.

Title: Self as coach, self as leader : developing the best in you to develop the best in
  others / Pamela McLean.

Description: Sixth Edition. | Hoboken : Wiley, 2019. | Includes index. |
  Identifiers: LCCN 2019005880 (print) | LCCN 2019006631 (ebook) | ISBN
  9781119562542 (Adobe PDF) | ISBN 9781119562573 (ePub) | ISBN 9781119562559
  (hardback)

Subjects: LCSH: Employees–Counseling of–Handbooks, manuals, etc. |
  Employees–Coaching of–Handbooks, manuals, etc. | Personnel
  management–Handbooks, manuals, etc. | Mentoring in business–Handbooks,
  manuals, etc. | BISAC: BUSINESS & ECONOMICS / Industries / General. |
  BUSINESS & ECONOMICS / Leadership.

Classification: LCC HF5549.5.C8 (ebook) | LCC HF5549.5.C8 H83 2019 (print) |
  DDC 658.3/124–dc23

LC record available at https://lccn.loc.gov/2019005880

Printed in the United States of America

V10009180 040219

*To my late grandmother, Margaret D. McLean,
a model of courage, creativity and love.*

*To my three sons, Christopher, Michael, and Charles,
my best teachers in life.*

CONTENTS

FOREWORD

Over the years, I have spoken at many international coaching conferences and been struck by the number of coaches eagerly searching for new tools and methods from the panoply of workshops on offer, while ignoring the most important tool and resource they need for their work, namely their own self.

All leadership happens through relationship, and the same is even more true of coaching. "It takes two to tango" and "it takes two to coach." Rather than think that as coaches we are coaching the client, it would be better to think of how we are doing the coaching in partnership between the coachee and coach, facing the challenges and lessons that life is providing for the client. This requires us to listen, not just with our ears and our neocortex, to understand cognitively what the client is relating to us, but also to listen with our whole body, to listen verbally and non-verbally, to the lyrics and the harmonics, to what is in the story and in the room and what is excluded, not in the room, but needs to be invited in. This may include the wider stakeholders of the client, needs from the future, or shadow aspects of the client. As coaches, we need to be resonating echo chambers that are finely tuned to the faintest of signals, both from the client as well as from their wider stakeholder ecosystem. This requires a lifetime of practice, supervision, and discipline, where we not only develop a depth of empathy and compassion with the individual client, but also "wide-angled empathy" for every individual, team, and system in their story (Hawkins, 2018).

It is with this in mind that I was delighted to receive and read Pam McLean's latest book, in which she generously offers her long experience of coaching, supervising, and training coaches, to how we can use all of our self, in service of the work of coaching others. She offers not only powerful disciplines and practices we can use to regularly tune up our self as instrument, but also stories from her own life's journey and vignettes of work with clients, illustrating how she has applied her deepening sensitivity. This weaving by Pam of the various strands illustrates how coaching is not something you can just learn in an initial training and then apply, but rather a lifelong action learning journey, where the challenges and learnings that are brought to you by your clients, if attended to with quality reflection, deepen and hone your practice, help you unlearn your previous models and assumptions, and deepen your *self as instrument* in service of others.

Pam McLean has been a beacon in the American coaching landscape, quietly showing how quality supervision is essential in this lifetime journey of deepening your self to deepen your coaching. For many cultural, political, legal, and historical reasons, the United States has been slower than many other parts of the world to adopt and develop the importance of lifelong learning and supervision for coaches (Hawkins & Smith, 2013; Hawkins & Turner, 2017). The Hudson Institute of Coaching in Santa Barbara, which Pam leads and where she teaches, has not just built supervision into all their training courses, but has also developed a supervision and lifelong learning ethic into their alumni community. In this book, in her own quiet and clear way, Pam provides a whole book showing the essential ingredients of our internal landscape, which details the qualities we need to constantly refine and deepen to be an effective coach. She shows that to develop these qualities requires more than self-reflection; the mirror, echo-resonance, support, and challenge of others and particularly trained supervisors who are further down the path than ourselves is an important component, as well.

I would recommend this book to all coaches, wherever they are on their coaching journeys, for even those of us who have been coaching for many decades need to have a beginner's mind that is learning afresh with each client relationship and a practice of daily tuning of the instrument of our being to deeper and more subtle levels of receptivity and resonance.

Professor Peter Hawkins
Author of *Leadership Team Coaching* and many other
coaching and leadership-related books

PREFACE

to produce
effect
lacking
shape or form
efficiency

The Completely Revised Handbook of Coaching was written in 2012. This is where Self as Coach was first written about. Until then, we had regularly referred to the concept of going deeper and attending to what's beneath the surface in order to create the conditions for real change to occur, but until 2012, it was an amorphous concept. In the intervening years, I have used Self as Coach in my work at the Hudson Institute, training coaches and coach supervisors. This has given me the opportunity to research and test the efficacy and value of the model. Through time, experience, and study, the model has evolved in some important ways: I have broadened and deepened the dimensions, acknowledged the interplays and overlaps, and emphasized the fluidity of the model from interaction to interaction.

Our findings provide ample evidence that there is real value in providing coaches and leaders with a simple path into exploring one's internal landscape. This landscape accentuates the reality that our ability to use our "self" as the most important instrument in our work is paramount. As coaches and leaders, we need a roadmap that allows us to combine our horizontal and vertical development. We need a means to make the very best use of our self as our most important resource when working in this highly charged relationship domain.

Of course, it's impossible to write a book exploring one's internal landscape without paying attention to my own changing landscape. I have sought to use my reflections and experiences in a transparent way in this book in order to provide a personal voice that might breathe life into these concepts in ways that are useful to the reader.

My goal in writing this is simple: to help us, as coaches and leaders, make the leap from *good enough* to *truly great*—coaches and leaders who are able to understand our inner gifts and the challenges in the service of building breadth of capacity. We need this breadth to meet the broad spectrum of issues and challenges confronted by the leaders we coach. Well-honed skills, soaring IQs, and impressive credentials are insufficient for us to do our best work. The ability to create the conditions to explore what's below the surface provides the possibility for deeper change to occur: change that transforms us as leaders and allows us to do our best work.

ACKNOWLEDGMENTS

[handwritten annotation: the force that makes something happen]

Writing a book is in the domain of deep work—a solitary, maddening, and joyful undertaking. Yet, it is never created in isolation. This book represents the work and influence of many people and the most important contributors are the hundreds and hundreds of leaders and coaches I have had the privilege of working with over the past 30 years. Everything I have learned from them is the impetus for this work and what makes it possible.

I am most appreciative to all those who read parts or all of the manuscript and provided feedback that both challenged and affirmed my thinking along the way: Toni McLean, Bev Kaye, Pat Adson, John Schuster, Steve Milovich, Tom Pollack, Ana Pliopas, Leslie Goldenberg, and Bill Lindberg.

To everyone at Wiley who helped make this possible—Jeanenne Ray and Vicki Adang—thank you for believing this subject is an important one! To my talented development editor, Nat Chen, who is masterful at her craft. I am grateful she was willing to travel with me on yet another book project. My work is simply better in every way because of her. To Amy Detrick, who created all of the illustrations, I owe you a special debt for making the book more meaningful and approachable.

INTRODUCTION

Leaping into the Dark Woods

In the middle of the journey of our life
I found myself astray in a dark wood
where the straight road had been lost sight of.
— *Dante Alighieri, The Inferno*

THE CULTIVATION OF THE COACH'S
INTERNAL LANDSCAPE

William James, professor of philosophy and psychology at Harvard early in the twentieth century, wrote about "once-born" and "twice-born" people (1913). He described once-borns as those who tend not to veer very far off course in this life, staying close to who they believe they are or ought to be and what they think others expect of them. Once-borns may not be fully satisfied with their lives, but they choose not to venture into the shadowy "woods," that mysterious territory where the unknown surpasses the predictable. Twice-born people, through choice or crisis, cross into the woods (sometimes with no alternative and other times willingly), make mistakes, allow themselves to fully suffer losses, learn from them, and get up again. These people are more likely to take a dive into exploring changes they need to make in themselves in order to live a life that radiates with greater meaning, to reinvent themselves and shed old stories and ways of being to discover the new. A century earlier, Danish philosopher Kierkegaard used a similar analogy, a leap of faith or an inwardness, again underlining that willingness to veer off the road and into the woods when we don't know what is ahead. A century later, in today's world, to remain where it is safe has less appeal and is simply insufficient if we want to live a life of meaning.

Every so often in life, an unforeseen leap presents itself, opening the way to dark woods that are mysterious and unwelcoming and yet there is no way to turn back on the path. I include lines from *The Inferno* as the opening of this introduction because Dante's chronicling of his journey through hell and into paradise provides rich metaphorical ground for understanding life's surprises and losses. First, we enter the dark woods, and then we find a light that guides us to a new time, a new place, and even a deeper way of being. Dante's epic story reminds us that even without adequate preparation or a view of what's ahead, something unfolds that changes one's life forever. This is an experience we all collide with at some point along our journey if we are willing to step into that second-born space, knowing that sometimes we step in prepared and welcoming, and other times tentative and fearful.

I stood at the edge of those unwelcoming woods midway through my adult journey and the unfolding experience of suddenly entering uncharted territory led me into a twice-born experience, changing me and my philosophy of life. Just as I was leaving my 40s and reveling in what felt like a perfect life—a great family of three beautiful boys, a loving marriage of many years, and satisfying and meaningful work— our whole family was confronted with a challenging upheaval. It was one of those turning points in life none of us would willingly invite and yet there was simply no turning back.

In Dante's words, I had to step into the dark woods where the straight line was lost, with no sense of the way out. The upheaval, which was my version of the leap into the woods, was my husband's diagnosis of early-onset Alzheimer's. At that time, we had three active and growing children, and a business still very much in the early stages. We reveled in all of the usual future dreams and plans (the "somedays") and suddenly our perfect life was gone. Like many others, my leap into a twice-born state was mandatory more than cou- rageous. Yet, the results were likely much the same: a new way of being in a world turned upside down, a new version of myself, and a new perspective on a life forever shifted.

This particular leap evolved over time, sometimes slowly and at other times with a pace that was difficult to keep step with. In the early stages, I was in shock, followed by anger and questions like "why me?" and "why our family?" Eventually, I came to understand that this is life. It's not what happens because "stuff happens!" It is how I live into it with grace and courage that matters most. It was definitely one of those rare twice-born experiences that has had a significant influence on my view of life, the world, and my work. As a coach, it has taught me endless lessons, including how much deep listening makes a difference, how sympathy is never as helpful as empathy, and the reality that some issues and challenges in our lives are not solvable, but rather are situations we must live into in new ways.

LEARNING TO BE "TWICE BORN": LEADERS WHO KNOW THEMSELVES AND THE COACHES THEY NEED

Much has changed in our world since James conceived of once- and twice-born lives. In today's complicated and rapidly evolving world, it seems to demand that we all become twice- and likely thrice-born, if not more! It is almost impossible for us to flourish as human beings, leaders, and organizations if we remain once-born, which is defined by lacking the courage to take a leap, see dilemmas from new perspectives, challenge our most cherished assumptions and preferences, test new approaches, and cultivate innovation. How do we consciously avoid the once-born worldview and instead embrace a way of being in which we do all of these things?

Some of this path from once-born to twice-born and beyond is a very personal inner journey that requires saying yes to the unknown, to unearthing our particular well-worn beliefs, and acknowledging and then wandering away from stories that keep us comfortably locked in an invisible set of habits and constraints. Other parts of the path to twice-born lie in all that is external to us. These parts require examining and saying yes and no to the myriad of complicated global issues impacting all of us. Our world today demands a twice-born approach at a grander and broader professional and community level than ever before if we are to survive, thrive, and fully face troubling global challenges on all fronts.

As coaches working in the world of leadership, if we want to engage in the kind of coaching that creates relevant change, we will need to operate differently than we did when leadership coaching first emerged as a field 30 years ago. We will need to reach well beyond a predictable toolkit of skill-based competencies and practiced inquiries to coach the growing number of twice-born leaders the changing world now needs and demands. Today's leaders are confronting challenges far more complex than in the past and at a speed that is vastly more pressing. Great coaches need far more agility and breadth of capacities than ever before to operate successfully in this new environment.

LEADERS WHO KNOW THEMSELVES

> The higher executives climb on the organizational ladder, the less they can depend on technical skills and the greater their need for effective interpersonal skills and emotional intelligence.
> —*Manfred Kets de Vries (2014)*

True leaders today need far more than strategies and smarts—the IQ of leadership. Today's leaders need to know themselves—their blind spots, values, possibilities, patterns, and old stories. They need to know how to be team players, to think and engage the collective leadership of those around them. This is the We-Q work of today and represents the need to shift from our long-held individualistic orientation to one that recognizes broader systems and acknowledges this truth: that the "leader as hero" model and command-and-control orientation are largely remnants of the past. In today's world, the price of counterproductive leadership behavior is unimaginably costly and even the best of leaders face challenges that are daunting. The coaches equipped to successfully work with leaders in these changing times need nimbleness, understanding of complexities, ease with ambiguities, and deep familiarity with their own internal landscape.

uncertainty

THE COACHES THEY NEED

Like everything else in our world, the field of coaching is changing dramatically. Timothy Gallwey's well-known *The Inner Game of Tennis* (1974) was a precursor to the early days of coaching. Written in the mid-1970s, Gallwey drew our attention to the psychological interference, or "self-talk," that goes on inside our heads, impacting performance both on the tennis court and off. His work stirred the world of mentoring and sparked the early rumblings of coaching. It was followed in the mid-1980s by John Whitmore's *Coaching for Performance.*

Yet, well into the 1990s, the growth of coaching was slow. When my late husband, Frederic Hudson, published *The Handbook of Coaching* in 1999, there were only a small handful of books written about this emerging field and there was little clarity about precisely what coaching represented. Was it a conversation? Was it focused on business, life, development, problems, goals, or searching? I recall that most often, when we would describe ourselves as coaches, people would immediately inquire, what sport? As coaching found its way into organizations in those early years, it was too often used as a "red card"—the leader with a coach was a leader in trouble.

A little more than 10 years later, when I did a major rewrite on *The Handbook of Coaching*, the coaching landscape had changed dramatically to include hundreds of books on the market, a growing body of research and doctoral dissertations, and a shift in the United States from the early days of five or six coaching schools to well over 500. Today, coaching is a multibillion-dollar business that, like so many other professions, risks decline if we continue to operate in a business-as-usual mentality.

Our traditional focus on the individualistically crafted goal(s) of the leader who we support, through a classic coaching engagement, is no longer sufficient. The early bias assumed that "a coach is a coach" and background didn't matter because a skilled coach would be able to do great coaching with anyone. We know today this simply is not the case. Those of us coaching senior leaders need to understand organizational systems, the field of leadership, the challenges of today's world of work, and the volatile world in which we live. The old belief that a good coach can coach anyone no longer holds up.

The traditional approach to developing coaches has relied heavily on skill-based competencies. While these are important, they are simply insufficient preparation for a coach to be masterful in their work. Leadership coaching has matured considerably over the past decade and we have many good coaches today. However, to excel as a discipline, we need to consciously raise the bar, cultivating great coaches able to do far more than listen well and ask questions. We need coaches who are adept in systems thinking, equipped to explore complex and ambiguous issues, and able to move with nimbleness and responsiveness based on the leader's needs. Unless we are willing to take certain leaps and move into the next chapter of the field of coaching, we will fall short. If we fall short, we will cease to exist as a discipline.

My own entry into the field of coaching tracks to the field's evolution of "coaching then" and "coaching now." My career path began after my doctoral work; I actively practiced as a clinical and organizational psychologist for two decades in which I deepened my understanding of the interplay between one's internal landscape and the complexities of the systems in which we exist. The second half of my career led me into the field of leadership coaching when this emerging field was in its infancy. At that time, leadership coaching was broad and a little ambiguous, ranging from short-term work tactically focused in the moment to longer-term work concentrated on deeper themes that ultimately created developmental shifts for the individual.

Given my immersion in the field of psychology, I was particularly interested then, and remain interested today, in coaching that is, by nature, developmental and focused on supporting someone in making changes that shift their way of being as a leader and as a human being. That is what inspired my own work in earlier chapters of The Completely Revised Handbook of Coaching (2012) and it is that developmental focus integrated with a coaching approach that seems most needed in the demanding lives of leaders in our rapidly changing world today.

In the early days of coaching, there was almost a singular focus on a set of solely skill-based competencies, a belief anyone could coach anyone, and woefully insufficient attention to the internal cultivation of a coach that would allow for true developmental work to occur—the kind that supports deeper changes.

Our roots at Hudson are embedded in the developmental areas of the human, the adult, and the life course, intertwined with philosophical underpinnings and a psychological perspective. We continually focus on broadening the view of leadership coaching and infusing a developmental orientation to the work of the coach. In our complex world today, this deeper, more transformative developmental work is even more relevant than it was in more predictable and stable times. Much is demanded of today's leaders and much is required. In addition to the standard competencies, today's leaders need clarity of purpose, courage, and a deeper self-awareness than ever before. Today, we understand that the cultivation of the coach's internal landscape is necessitated and made mutually powerful by a cultural moment that demands a similar inward-looking approach to leadership.

THE LEAP FOR THE ORGANIZATION

All leaders know well they are living in new times that are unpredictable, chaotic, and constantly shifting. The U.S. Army War College dubbed this VUCA (volatility, uncertainty, complexity, and ambiguity), and others have expanded this definition to Super-VUCA to underline the dramatic forces at play today. Change is our most predictable constant, unfolding at an ever-increasing speed and seldom revealing a path forward as clear and straightforward as it once was. This new climate of rapid change also leads to expected as well as unexpected leaps forward for the organization.

Given these conditions, one fact we are all clear on is that our most precious commodity is our human capital and our greatest challenge is cultivating, developing, and retaining great talent in our organizations in tumultuous and unpredictable times.

What does this require? It requires organizations to be crystal clear about their vision, mission, and place in the world. It requires an all-out commitment to developing people and an ability to do so both on the spot, in the moment, as well as over the length of their career paths. It requires leaders who have sharper sensibilities about the needs and motivations of today's workforce and world. The world of work is undergoing massive change; the days of leaders seeking long-term, secure employment with one firm or organization is largely gone; and the view of the skills and talents that are most needed is continually shifting. What does all of this mean for us? Simply put, it means the needs of organizations and leaders are radically changing. In such an environment, the paramount indicator of success for an organization is the ability to aid a leader at any level to be at their best—in a way that improves both full engagement and impact—as quickly as possible. In Gallwey's language, the work is in supporting the leader to find their inner game in order to be at their best.

TODAY'S LEADERS NEED COACHES WHO HAVE THEIR OWN INNER GAME

The needs of our clients in the realm of leadership coaching is continually changing as the VUCA world unfolds. Our challenge is to reliably develop leaders both in the moment and over the course of their careers inside today's complex systems, organizational structures, and constantly shifting realities of the larger world. Leadership coaching with a developmental focus is not centered on solving problems or providing shortsighted quick fixes. Instead, developmental coaching helps leaders identify and undertake changes that will allow them to be even more effective in their roles and in their systems with a view and linkage to the needs of the broader world, thus using more of themselves in all of their roles by consciously cultivating their inner capacities. This work requires exploration of all that lies beneath the surface. It requires a depth of knowledge and capacity from a coach who is willing to continuously evolve in their work, as well.

Entering this domain and operating masterfully as a coach requires far more than a quiver of knowledge, skills, and tools. And while our current climate allows anyone to hang out a coaching shingle as a leadership or executive coach where often the primary focus is creating a brand, a marketing plan, and a network; on the upside, the field is maturing, research is growing, and those dedicated to the art and science of coaching continue to raise the bar. Leaders deserve great coaches and great coaches need a quiver that contains skills, tools, methods, practices, and the ability to cultivate and use one's self.

Masterful coaching requires something quite different. I believe for leadership and executive coaching to thrive, we need to expand our breadth of knowledge and our depth of capacity beyond our current state in order to be of help to leaders who are dealing with increasingly complex, wicked[1] challenges at a speed not experienced before. Engaging in a developmental approach in coaching requires a focus

---

[1] Originally used in social planning, it has come to denote issues resistant to resolution.

on deep change and deeper understanding, working nimbly inside complex systems, and attention to:

- Understanding rather than telling.
- Seeking rather than arriving.
- Complexity rather than linear singularity.
- Systemic thinking rather than individualistic thinking.
- Provoking and sharing observations rather than relying exclusively on inquiry-based approaches.
- Cultivating capacity for polarity as well as "yes, and" thinking.
- Prioritizing justice and mercy, consistency and innovation.
- Developing a deep ethical compass based on values.

different thinking

A coach simply cannot do this developmental work without first beginning at home, by thoroughly exploring, understanding, and deepening the internal landscape of one's own self, before proceeding to coach others. We grow our capacity to operate masterfully by first gaining a true sense of the self we are living in. This is not the journey all coaches will choose, but if the path of engaging in deep developmental coaching of leaders is one you decide you want to travel, then this book offers a window into how we grow and develop our self in order to become capable of supporting others in this deeper journey.

ABOUT THIS BOOK

This book builds upon *The Completely Revised Handbook of Coaching* I wrote in 2012, by extending the guidance of the handbook to a deeper and more longitudinal look at the formation of a coach via coaching: not just how coaches learn their craft, but how they are made and changed by coaching itself. It is intended primarily for leadership coaches willing to take a leap and invest in deepening the quality and capacity of their work with clients. It is also meant for any coach who is fully committed to the ongoing and rigorous development of their inner selves, understanding that the strength and quality of our work with others is directly proportionate to our understanding and continual cultivation of self. It is meant for all coaches who are prepared to see beyond the individual client and comprehend the necessity of grasping the intricacies of all levels of our human systems.

This book takes an in-depth look at the internal landscape of a coach and all of the complexities and nuances we need to explore, cultivate, and continually re-examine in order to keep our saw sharp. I examine this internal landscape through six broad dimensions of our interior knowing that overlap and support one another: presence, empathy, range of feelings, boundaries and systems, embodiment, and courage.

I spend time in the early chapters revisiting foundational concepts that are essential grounding territory for a developmental coach, and I seek to add unexplored dimensions to these concepts through stories and examples from my own journey as a coach. A great leadership coach gains considerably by understanding well-known concepts in the fields of neo-analytic psychology, attachment theories, object relations, as well as contemporary concepts and strains in leadership theory, organizational development, and neuroscience.

This book has four distinct but complementary elements:

1. Reflections on my journey as a coach through several theoretical foundations for a broad view of self (Chapters 1 and 2)
2. Six dimensions of my Self as Coach model (Chapters 3 through 9), including opportunities to reflect, engage in practices, and develop one's own roadmap for development
3. Three *Applying Heat* interchapters that use case vignettes to illustrate the complexities of Self as Coach as it is lived and practiced
4. Two final chapters focused on the application of Self as Coach in coach supervision and in the Self as Leader (Chapters 10 and 11)

For the purposes of this book, *coachee* and *leader* are interchangeable. I frequently refer to leaders being coached as *coachee* when they are being portrayed in a vignette or discussed in terms of the setting of a coaching engagement.

WHO IS THIS BOOK FOR?

- *Coach Practitioners:* For all who are seriously committed to providing coaching that supports growth, depth, and meaning for leaders in today's complex world, this book provides an in-depth exploration of the full use of self that opens the way to looking *beneath the surface* in our work, in support of skillful and masterful coaching.

- *Mentors:* For those building mentoring programs within organizations, this book provides a look at key areas of the self that enables a mentor to cultivate the conversations that will help them guide the growth of another leader.
- *Leaders:* Like coaches, great leaders today need to *know thyself,* and the Self as Coach model can easily be translated into Self as Leader. The self-awareness of a leader is perhaps one of the greatest differentiators for anyone stepping into a significant leadership role. This book maps the internal dimensions of the self in a manner that links to the daily challenges leaders at all levels face.
- *Educators and Providers of Coach Training:* For all those providing coach training in a structured certification program or those teaching coaching skills in an academic setting within a business school or inside executive education programs, this book offers a careful examination of what's required in order to fully utilize one's self as the most important instrument in the coaching engagement.

Chapter 1

THE COACH'S INTERNAL LANDSCAPE IS ESSENTIAL DEVELOPMENT TERRITORY

> The hardest thing to attend to is that which is closest to
> ourselves, that which is most constant and familiar.
> And this closest something is ourselves, our own habits and
> ways of being and ways of doing things.
> —*John Dewey, American philosopher*

When someone decides to become a coach, it requires taking a leap into new territories because the work of a coach challenges much of what has always felt natural and normal in our conversations. An early hurdle is the difficulty of stepping back from the notion that coaching is about solving problems. It is assumed that a good coach has the answers and should be armed and ready to leap into the mode of "telling." This is not coaching. It might be advising or consulting; it might be mentoring; and it is surely satisfying for those who love their answers, but it is not coaching. Another hurdle is letting go of the notion that the most effective coaching happens in a sacred and secure vacuum between coach and client. Exploration and experimentation of new ways of being, in isolation, does not support change. In fact, it stunts change! Our most effective work happens when we embrace a systemic approach that invites the voices of all stakeholders into the coaching process and additionally asks those stakeholders to play a role and take responsibility for their parts in the work of the coaching. This approach is more complex for the coach and requires careful attention to seeing all layers of the system in order to yield an impact that is much greater and deeper.

Yet another hurdle is the reality that our clients are ill-served by coaches creating a safe and cozy space for the work. Instead, we need to create space that is most definitely safe, but with enough tension and heat that the most effective work can happen. Without some heat, we can end up making the coaching space so comfy nothing happens or so cozy that we are actually colluding with the client to keep the status quo alive.

What do I mean by "heat"? Heat is created when we are fully present to what is happening in the moment, using "what's in the room" transparently rather than intellectualizing and "talking about." Nick Petrie (2015) writes about what constitutes heat in reference to the vertical development of a leader. He suggests heat requires new experiences where results matter: there is a chance of success and failure, important people are watching, and the experience is extremely uncomfortable. Many of these conditions are at play when we create a milieu that is both safe and heated.

And, finally, we must realize that our work in coaching is far more than asking questions. Yes, we need great skills in inquiry that will serve our clients, but inquiry is insufficient to support the development of another person in areas that matter. We need to share observations and patterns, challenge old beliefs, use what's in the room, and have the courage to enter uncharted territory, even when it is going to be a little uncomfortable.

LEAPING FORWARD IN THE FIELD OF COACHING

These are just some of the leaps that allow us to step into the future of coaching and, in particular, into a deeply developmental approach to coaching that embraces the entire system. There is one more leap that coaching, particularly U.S.-based coaching, has not sufficiently embraced. This last leap is the wisdom we can gain from having a basic understanding of the psychological dimensions of the human being. Becoming a great developmental coach demands a grasp of the vast body of knowledge that exists around this field of study as it informs and intertwines with our own best work as coaches. Without this knowledge, we are insufficiently equipped to understand layers of our own humanness as well as the psychological dimensions of our clients. Such an understanding provides helpful insights and shifts our approaches and interventions along the way.

The cultivation of our internal landscape is some of the most important work we need to invest in for our continual development as a coach. Many of us come to coaching imagining all we need in order to get started on this path are some skill-based competencies, a few tools, and a set of techniques to support our work.

The truth is, we need more than just the known essentials. We need knowledge, skill competencies, and a solid methodology to do our work. Some key tools and practices are also important. However, all of these requirements are insufficient in order for us to be at our best as great developmental coaches. If we are aware and observant, we get a wake-up call early in our journey as coaches, a bit of a rude awakening as we bump into the reality that the greatest tool we need to cultivate is our self. What's more, to know one's self requires a fierce and courageous willingness to explore the many layers of one's inner landscape, a territory that can be elusive and enigmatic, confusing and paradoxical. This space can be intimidating if we have not spent much time there.

There are many professions and fields of study where cultivating an understanding of one's self is not required work. This is not true in the profession of coaching. In coaching, our work is deeply relational. This reality necessitates that we thoroughly engage in honing the greatest, most versatile tool we possess as coach—our self. This means the whole, cultivated, managed self that we bring to the work of coaching to inspire and help effect change.

So where does a coach begin in this exploration? What does this ambiguous phrase inner landscape entail? How do I examine the many parts of myself? What maps and guides might be helpful as I begin this exploration or even dive deeper into an exploration that is already well underway? These are questions that most of us have asked. To get us started on this journey, we can look to a handful of primary and enduring theories that serve as helpful grounding for our understanding of the internal landscape in broad terms.

I have shaped an anchor for us from several foundational works that have examined the study of the self over many decades and through many theoretical perspectives. In order to illustrate the depth and impact of those perspectives on the life of a coach, I offer up some of my own personal experiences of the concepts and phenomena described by these perspectives. These vignettes of my earlier years and my making as a coach are meant to be reminders of how theories don't just live in the head but how we, as coaches, embody them all the time.

In Chapter 2, I begin by exploring key aspects of Karen Horney's neo-analytic perspective, then turn to Bowlby's well-known work on attachment theory, move to Kegan's self-object work on the developmental stages of the adult journey, and conclude the chapter examining Petrie's concept of vertical and horizontal development. Each of these theorists provides a useful vantage point that is both broad and rich in meaning and aptly applies to us as coach as well as to our work with our clients. Throughout the sections, I offer myself up as an example of a coach learning this work and as a human being living these concepts. At the conclusion of each section, I offer a short series of questions for those who would like to use this book as a tool for their own exploration of self.

Chapter 2

FOUNDATIONAL WORKS INFORMING OUR INTERNAL LANDSCAPE

*We think we tell stories, but stories often tell us, tell us to love
or hate, to see or be seen. Often, too often, stories saddle us,
ride us, whip us onward, tell us what to do, and we do it
without questioning.*
*The task of learning to be free requires learning to hear them,
to question them, to pause and hear silence, to name them,
and then become a story-teller.*
—*Rebecca Solnit (2014)*

We tell stories and our stories tell us. One of my stories is about my grandparents emigrating from Scotland at the turn of the twentieth century. They left their home country out of desperation with impending signs of starvation, arriving on a new continent well before immigration laws were in place. They ventured to a new country of which they had virtually no knowledge and ultimately homesteaded the farm and cattle ranch I grew up on nestled at the corner of Manitoba, Minnesota, and North Dakota. They were courageous, rugged, resourceful and family focused. In spite of the inevitable losses that come with the upheaval of immigrating to a new land, they managed to arrive with optimism, determination, and their rich cultural history (including bagpipes!) to sustain them. Like everyone, my history reaches back much farther than a generation. Our roots run deep and they provide added texture to our family and a breadth of context for our individual lives. My Scottish heritage is embedded in the long-standing McLean Clan, one of the oldest Gaelic clans of Scotland, both brutish and brave. Because of this rich history, a love of the land, a strong work ethic, and a family focus run deep in me. I step outside my home today overlooking a vast canyon that is home to coyotes, hawks, owls, and bobcats, and I feel at home, at ease in the rhythms of nature that are a part of my heritage and in my bones.

During my growing-up years in rural America, I could see for miles across a prairie both wild and tamed. The post-World War II mood was very much present in my early years and my parents' growing-up memories were etched with experiences and memories of both World War II and The Great Depression. Rural life in the 1950s was isolated, family-focused, and hard-working, buoyed by a new time in history, filled with opportunity and social constraints and perhaps an under-standable attention to fitting in, looking good, and doing good. Diver-sity was found in the customs, religious practices, and beliefs that were brought from the European countries from which most homesteaders originated. This is one of my deeply rooted stories.

The links connecting our past to our present are powerful and enduring in the lives of each of us. The earliest behavior patterns etched into our beings shape our adult lives as we repeat those behav-ior patterns in important relationships at home and at work. As long as we are blind to these connections and patterns, we are held hostage, faced with limitations in our interactions and in our interpretation of the world's many layers of relationships. Even today, with thorough awareness, this story of my roots impacts my coaching and how I move in the world and in my work. Even with practiced awareness, this is what our stories do.

This chapter examines a handful of foundational works providing windows into the shaping of our earliest years through our primary relationships. Exploring this territory as a coach provides us with in-sight and compassion into our own roots and subsequent behavioral patterns. It also helps us loosen the grip on patterns that were born out of circumstances and a drive to survive—patterns that today limit us and at times confound the relationships that are most important to us. As always, as coaches we start at home. In so doing, we gain a better understanding and appreciation for those with whom we work.

OUR SCRIPTS AND STORIES

We each come to our stories and scripts through our experiences growing up and the adaptations that, in most cases, we wisely made to adjust and thrive in our family dynamics at that time in our lives. Trouble is, we continue to practice those adaptations and adjustments well into our adult lives when often they become ineffectual, leaving our current relationships inevitably tinged and shaded by our earliest relationships. As you continue to read about these perspectives—Horney's home bases, Bowlby's attachment styles, Kegan's levels of development, and Petrie's concept of vertical and horizontal development—you'll likely self-identify some of the adaptations you made to thrive in your family system and you'll probably quickly land on what is home and habit for you in each. Weaving all these perspectives together begins to stitch together a complex story and our insights provide a deeper understanding of our internal landscape. This draws us closer to appreciating the origins of our stories and those of our clients. We all come by our stories and our interpretation of the world through the lives we've led and particularly through the earliest formative years of our development. Yes, we are capable of adjusting the landscape, and reworking the frameworks, but first we have to *see* them!

We begin by exploring the three home bases developed by Karen Horney, then we move on to the important work of Bowlby's attachment theory, and from these earliest experiences in life that mold us, examine how we develop through our adult years. This chapter represents far more than an academic foray into theory. Get ready to take this personally, examine aspects of your internal landscape with fresh eyes, challenge yourself to discover territory that you have left largely uncultivated, and be willing to be surprised!

There are case examples and questions posed throughout for your personal exploration, a "Coach's Worksheet" accessible online, which serves as an opportunity to routinely step back from each chapter and reflect on what meaning it has for you and what practices you might develop to keep honing your capacity as coach. There are also pieces called "My Inner Landscape" that serve as a kind of journal of my own inner work to process what I have learned from each of the foundational theorists explored in this chapter. These are moments of my own feelings of being challenged and surprised, which I hope will serve as testament to the idea that taking it personally is often the best way to understand and internalize some of these foundational concepts.

NEO-ANALYTIC PERSPECTIVE FROM KAREN HORNEY: LIFE'S ENDURING STANCES

Karen Horney's neo-analytic work (1945) examining our basic neurotic strategies, while deeply psychological, provides a useful starting point when examining the broad expanse of our internal terrain. Her work examines social relationships and the interpersonal conflict that arises in our lives. She posits a triangle of coping strategies that I have adapted for our purposes to include three relatively enduring stances in life for most of us: Moving Away, Moving Against, and Moving Toward. Those of us with a "moving away" stance will be likely to step back more often than lean in whether the situation is casual or conflictual. This is simply the comfort zone that has been honed out of the past and is now a dominant way of being. Those among us with a "moving against" stance will do the opposite: leaning in to challenge and sharing observations even when uninvited or unnecessary and exhibiting a pushing energy in interactions with others. Those in the "moving toward" stance will lean in instead of challenging, working to connect through caring about and for others, oftentimes overdoing the caring and veering into the territory of collusion.

At a high level, Horney's three-part model shown in Figure 2.1 provides a broad brushstroke for our internal landscape. Horney posits that each of us has a home base we find most reassuring and comforting, a stance that is thoroughly known to us. Our home base has been well cultivated through our earliest attachment experiences in childhood, and the stories and experiences in our early years often shape those realities in our adult lives. This home base and the stories we live into have the profound potential to drive our lives when left unexamined. Horney's work spans the continuum from normal to neurotic defenses at play when varying degrees of family dysfunction are present in the child's life.

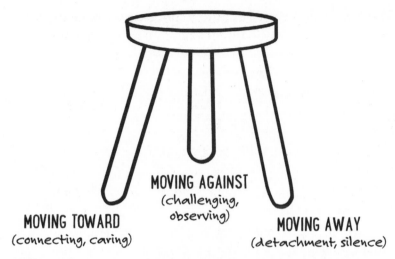

Figure 2.1 Horney's Moving Toward, Moving Against, Moving Away

For our purposes, we can examine her model through the lens of normal defenses. If we can step out "on the balcony" a bit to see our self using the lens she provides, we will gain a useful framework for coaching in the relationship systems we create with our clients. Each of the strategies of Moving Toward, Moving Against, and Moving Away has an upside and a downside, as shown in Table 2.1. At our best, it is optimal to have a sense of our familiar old home base and work to build practices that allow us to expand our agility and experience the other home bases, as well.

These three composite styles provide us with plenty of room to explore our internal landscape and determine how rooted we are in one of these home bases, which in turn helps us see where our own work might be in developing more agility.

From My Inner Landscape: What I Learned from Horney's Work

My own home base of Moving Away is one I honed in my early years. Now, as an adult, I consciously work to reshape and build new agility and ease in the other home bases, as well. Like everyone, my home base

Table 2.1 Characteristics of Moving Toward, Against, and Away

Moving Toward Characteristics	Moving Against Characteristics	Moving Away Characteristics
• Compliant • Helpless • Needing approval • Please others to be liked	• Hostile • Fighting against • Protection and revenge • Be the best to be liked	• Detached • Withdrawn • Isolating • Be self-sufficient to be liked
The Family Roots A child finds becoming overly compliant is the most likely way to receive the love and approval of parental figures.	**The Family Roots** A child finds fighting back and seeking to control through assertiveness is the most likely path to safety and security with parental figures.	**The Family Roots** A child detaches and disengages, relying on his/her own self-sufficiency in lieu of seeking the unpre-dictable love and approval of his/her parental figures.
The Upside • Caring • Connected	**The Upside** • Direct • Action focused	**The Upside** • Autonomous • Serene
The Downside • Seeking Approval • Compliant	**The Downside** • Overly Assertive • Seeking Recognition	**The Downside** • Overly Intellectual • Withdrawing Too Soon

was established when I was young. I consider myself fortunate to have had a mostly healthy family upbringing in a loving family. I grew up on a cattle ranch and wheat farm where we all worked hard, and the work seemed never-ending. My father was a true role model of steely heart, humility, and kindness, and he worked around the clock. My mother worked equally hard and was a perfectionist sprinkled with insecurities that led to the dreaded focus on *how we all appeared in the eyes of others*. This orientation mixed with a quick temper could lead to stormy disagreements and at times long periods of silence. Early on I figured out it was wisest to do a good job of managing myself in an attempt to stay out of the potential disagreements and silences. I wasn't always successful, but my strategy was likely smart at the time. This well-developed orientation of Moving Away in my youth requires conscious awareness on my part to reshape in my adult life, where it is no longer needed. As a coach and a leader of an organization, my ability to continually adapt and learn to Move Against and Move Toward with ease has been essential to my effectiveness as both a coach and a leader.

Horney in Coaching Engagements: Working from Different Home Bases

Read on and see if you are able to identify the home base you likely created in your early years.

Moving Toward

This composite has the powerful upside of almost instinctively knowing how to genuinely connect and create a working alliance with a coachee. Given that the working alliance and strong sense of empathy is the essential glue that makes all our work possible in coaching, this is a significant upside. What's more, caring comes naturally from this stance and it is readily apparent to one's coachee. The downside is a bit subtler and embedded in the urge to want to please the other and be liked by the other. This urge makes it tempting to be overly sympathetic and is often accompanied by a desire to rescue the leader or collude and get in the arena with the leader to help fix a situation. When the coach does this, they are not helping the leader to uncover blind spots and see themselves more clearly.

The following is a coaching example I have explored many times with coaches I work with. This case represents a composite of several engagements in which Horney's concept of Moving Toward is evidenced.

The Coach with a Moving Toward Home Base

Consider Jona, a coach most familiar with this stance of Moving Toward. She cares deeply about her client's challenging situation, in which the client describes suffering the daily challenges and anguishes of having "an impossible boss." As the coach, Jona is blinded a bit by her tendency to overcare, along with her familiar tug of wanting to be liked by her coachee. Jona finds herself colluding with her coachee and over-looking the opportunities to explore perspectives other than the coachee's belief that the problem is her tough boss. Jona feels a lot of compassion for this leader, because she remembers what it was like when she had a difficult boss herself. This makes her inclined to console instead of help the leader to explore all perspectives in her current situation.

Jona's natural inclination through Horney's lens is to Move Toward and the big upside of this orientation is her ease in creating a strong connection to her coachee. This is elemental in coaching and if Jona could combine this with some agility in other portions of the three home bases, she would be able to challenge the leader's thinking about her current situation without feeling as though she might risk offending. If Jona's only base is the Moving Toward stance, she'll likely find herself worrying that the coachee might pull back from the coaching or that the coachee will not like a message, observation, or provocative question that is anything but fully supportive of how she views her situation. So, the upside of Jona's stance is that it allows her to connect well and build a strong working alliance with her coachee; the downside is that she may become so connected that she loses her courage to share observations and patterns that may be important for this leader to consider.

Moving Against

Coaches at home in this territory have the great advantage of being fully at ease with directness and have a fully loaded focus on actionable next steps. These strengths are assets for the coach; the ability to be direct in ways that allow the leader to consider new perspectives is a big part of our value as coaches. The focus on actionable next steps is essential in our coaching work as we need to keep our eye on a finish line that satisfies the coaching goal(s). Those skilled at Moving Against are at home delivering the results. The downside of this stance is that, when overplayed, the coach can loosen one's grip on boundaries and move into a take charge and overly assertive space in which they are doing more. This, ultimately, may not serve the coachee's development.

The Coach with a Moving Against Home Base

Consider John, who is coaching Amir—a newly minted, C-Suite executive in a manufacturing industry where John has also had years of experience operating at the same level. John knows the ropes well and when his client, Amir, brings up an important project he needs to rapidly launch, John wants him to be successful and hit it out of the park. John worries about Amir's ability to do this because his stakeholder interviews revealed that one important focus of their coaching work would be centered on Amir's capacity to increase the velocity of his decision-making when the stakes are higher. At Amir's new level in the organization, the stakes are always higher! So, John leans into his natural stance of Moving Against and instead of managing his temptation to push and quickly move into "doing" mode, he becomes overly directive, getting ahead of Amir and creating a plan for success he thinks his client will benefit from and those in the organization would be impressed by.

Along the way, John loses his all-important connection with Amir, the connectedness that provides a sense that coach and leader are working together to co-create a path forward. In the end, Amir delivered the results that were needed in that instance, but he did so by following the plan his coach built instead of learning about himself and incorporating his new insights. Had he had the opportunity to do that, Amir would have also learned a new way of handling not only this situation but others that will inevitably arise as he continues in this role.

The upside of John's Moving Against stance is his willingness to be courageous and direct with his coachee, and when this is integrated with the other two stances it can become powerful ground from which the client can learn and grow. Yet, without that agility, the downside of this leg of the home bases is that too much directness without a strong connection can easily miss the mark with the client and leave John out ahead, touting his best thoughts and plans.

Moving Away

The coach at ease in this domain can create a container wherein they are comfortable stepping back to allow the client to sit in silence, staying in an important moment and reflecting and deepening a potential breakthrough moment. This ability to create more space for the client to sit in an intense moment, to reflect in the moment, can often be a true game-changer in deepening the coaching work. The downside of this stance is that, overplayed, this coach can create so much space there is a sense of not being attached enough to the relationship with the client.

The Coach with a Moving Away Home Base

Anya is coaching Marg, a very senior leader who oversees a large market responsible for generating a significant portion of the organization's annual revenues. Marg has had a history of meeting and exceeding her annual financial goals over the past several years and increasingly she has grown a reputation for meeting those revenue goals at the expense of good working relationships that foster strong teaming and a culture of collaboration. Anya is asked to coach Marg in order to help her find more effective ways of creating relationships with team members, with a goal of continuing to meet her financial targets in a shared way with her team through stronger collaboration and inclusiveness. Anya finds her client, Marg, to be extraordinarily bright, professional, and willing to enter into the coaching with a clear view of a goal that is important to her superiors and an agreement that this is a worthy focus in the coaching work.

Early in the coaching, Anya is able to create the space that allows Marg to make some powerful connections between the current state of her relationships with team members and her long history of an impersonal and remote style of relating that is heavily focused on goals she is pushing at the expense of a connectedness that breeds team togetherness. Anya's Moving Away stance has allowed her to "hold up the mirror" so Marg can see more clearly her old pattern. Yet once this breakthrough occurs, Anya steps back too far and leaves her client insufficiently practiced or able to move forward in new ways. If Anya had the agility to lean in when it served her client and help Marg build a tactical plan to practice a new way of being with her team, the outcome would be stronger.

In summary, if the habitual zone as coach is Moving Toward and the coach has little awareness of this in themselves, they will continually lean forward to comfort and rescue their clients, moving into their systems and stories and almost becoming a part of them. If Moving Against is the coach's comfort zone with little attunement, they will find themselves pushing their clients to action at a pace that works for the coach because they want to be recognized as adding value. Those in the Moving Away stance with insufficient awareness may pull back too far from their client, leaving the client with a sense of not being fully connected and engaged with the coach. At our best, we need to cultivate nimbleness and the ability to lean into all three stances at the right times when it is most needed.

OUT IN YOUR WORLD: HORNEY IN COACHING ENGAGEMENTS

What is your comfort zone and stance?

- Reflect on the life stories you return to that in many ways, define you. Explore connections between your root stories and examine which of these stories best describes how you move in the world as a coach or leader.

- Spend time reflecting on the roots of your stance, actively appreciating all that factored into this. Compassion for our root stances allows us to consciously grow and change.

- We are not static. Awareness mixed with motivation enables us to consciously adapt our stance over time. What adaptations have you already made and what are small adjustments that remain important in your work?

THE COACH'S WORKSHEET: DEVELOPING MORE RANGE

Visit www.selfascoach.com for an opportunity to and reflect on what meaning Horney's work has for you and what practices you might develop to keep honing your capacity as coach.

AN ATTACHMENT THEORY PERSPECTIVE FROM BOWLBY AND AINSWORTH

*Early mother-child interaction patterns determine the nature
and quality of present and future attachments.*
— Bowlby (1973)

Horney's broad mapping of the strategies we use for coping and our adaptation relative to our work as coach provides us with an overarching awareness of a general stance we developed over time. It also stimulates our awareness that these stances are rooted in our earliest years. This is an important connection for us to make as coaches. The experiences we have growing up invariably shape the stories and stances we live in much of, if not all of, our lives. The extent to which we adapt and update our stories and stances depends almost entirely upon our ability to see them. While our work as coach is not focused on deep-seated issues of one's childhood, the reality is that we all bring our childhood with us into our adulthood. This is good reason to understand this terrain and appreciate the origins of our longstanding stories and stances in life.

Bowlby (1973) helps us to understand the powerful imprint of our early attachment experiences on our adult lives. If you quickly scan close friendships and relationships in your life, you'll likely notice common signs that lead back to how attachments were created in the earliest of years. Most of us can identify someone in our life who is almost always confident, secure, and expecting good things to come of most situations, or the person who is most often a bit skeptical and fearful of trusting too much too soon, or the person who allows you to lean on them, but will seldom take advantage of leaning on another themselves. This is what attachment theory teaches us about and in so doing it provides us with another useful view into our internal landscape.

This body of research in developmental psychology extensively examines the patterns of connectedness and communication, often in the nonverbal interactions between parent and child in the earliest months and years, and reveals how these interactions mold the child's emotional and social development (Bowlby, 1973; Ainsworth, 1991). Bowlby and others stress that human beings have an enduring need for attachment and that the nature of our most formative attachment pattern will define, in any number of ways, how we live our lives.

Ainsworth's research found our attachments to be malleable when explored in the context of psychotherapy. The work of Bowlby and Ainsworth broadly led to three types of attachment: Secure, Ambivalent, and Avoidant. Years later, Main and Solomon (1986) discovered yet another type: Disorganized and Disoriented Attachment. While this newest addition is not as common and probably less relevant to the work of coaching, it is interesting in our current world, where we have over 60 million people around the globe living as refugees, to consider the attachment formed when the child's safe haven is actually a source of danger, or when the child experiences their parent as frightened—a state described by Main and Hesse (1990) as "fright without solution." For the purposes of coaching, let's briefly consider the three broad attachment styles outlined by Bowlby and modified by Ainsworth and leave Main and Solomon's contribution for others to examine.

Secure Attachment: This style occurs when the child has a consistent confidence that the attachment figure (traditionally, this is the mother) will be there to meet their needs. This creates a sense of security for the child who is borne into patterns of connectedness and communication throughout his or her life. This person finds the world to be a safe place, expects that interactions will be entered into with positive intent, and believes in the possibility of good outcomes.

Insecure-Avoidant Attachment: This style is the result of the child experiencing an attachment figure who is unavailable and potentially rejecting and insensitive to the child. This creates in the child an avoidance of connectedness and usually creates degrees of independence from the attachment figure. The person this child becomes may keep others at a distance and be inclined to maintain an overly independent position in interactions and relationships.

Insecure-Ambivalent Attachment: This style is rooted in the child's experience of the attachment figure being consistently inconsistent in their availability for connectedness and communication. This results in the child feeling ambivalent about attachment and often needy, dependent, and conflicted. This person is likely to be overly cautious and withholding of trust with most in his or her life.

Through the various attachment experiences with the primary parent(s) shown in Table 2.2—from the highly functional to the dysfunctional and everything in between—we learn how we need to adapt in order

Table 2.2 Attachment Experiences

Secure Attachment	Insecure Avoidant Attachment	Insecure Ambivalent Attachment
• Predictable and constant	• Rejecting verbally or physically	• Unpredictable, occasionally available
• Affirming	• Unavailable	• Withdrawn
• Ease in availability	• Insensitive	• Isolating
The Coach or Leader	**The Coach or Leader**	**The Coach or Leader**
• Secure	• Direct	• Withdrawn
• Available	• Cautious	• Cautious

to survive and potentially flourish. We develop a belief about human connectedness based on our early experiences, and our developing beliefs shape our relationships throughout our lives. This is true for us as coach and it is also true for the leaders with whom we work. Gaining a sense of our attachment style provides another lens into our internal landscape and a perspective on our clients, as well. Also, gaining an appreciation for the malleability of these styles in the medium of coaching, where we are able to observe and reflect, or in other reflective practices, provides a sense of agency and hopefulness about our ability to continue to grow and develop throughout our adult years.

From My Inner Landscape: What I Learned from Bowlby and Ainsworth's Work

In my work as a coach, I have found the backdrop of attachment theory to be enormously helpful. Starting with myself and understanding and appreciating my particular attachment style allows for the ability to manage myself, to hone what needs continual work, and to appreciate the reach that early attachments have in our lives. While my dominant experience in my early years is reflected in the secure attachment style, there are threads I can pull through from the avoidant style, as well, that I have continually worked on in order to be at my best as a coach. What I know is that when I am actively reflecting and attending to having my own self in order, I am able to see my client with more clarity, and I'm able to be present and listen through my client's eyes and heart rather than getting hooked by an old frame of reference in myself.

Bowlby in Coaching Engagements: Adjusting Our Attachment Styles

Our attachment style is developed early in life and the roots run deep. Just as in coaching, if we are awake to our style and the origins of our stance—our way of being in relation to others—we gain the capacity to make adjustments over time. The initial step on this path seems to be in our ability to acknowledge, grieve, and recover from early experiences that we may have locked away. This may not be what one would consider coaching work, but it surely is important work for a coach in order to be at our best in working with others.

OUT IN YOUR WORLD: LEARNING FROM THE WORK OF BOWLBY AND AINSWORTH

- As you reflect on these brief descriptions of attachment styles, what words and phrases get your attention?

- Might you spend some time amplifying the stories you hold about your early years to see what you might uncover?

- Upon reflection, do you have a sense of how you have adjusted your early script to cultivate the healthiest and most resilient you?

THE COACH'S WORKSHEET: DEVELOPING MORE RANGE

Visit www.selfascoach.com for an opportunity to step back and reflect on what meaning the work of Bowlby and Ainsworth has for you and what practices you might develop to keep honing your capacity as coach.

KEGAN'S STAGES OF DEVELOPMENT IN ADULTHOOD AND THE SELF-OBJECT DANCE

The frameworks of Horney, Bowlby, and Ainsworth provide sweeping views of the self, originating in the earliest years and profoundly impacting the entire course of the adult journey. Theories of our development spanning across the adult life also provide a useful backdrop for understanding our Self as Coach and our client. Kegan's theory of adult development provides a view into how we can continue to develop long after our early attachments are embedded. His constructive-developmental approach theory is focused on the meaning-making capacity of the individual rather than on an age or stage.

Kegan (1982) places particular emphasis on matters of authority, responsibility, and one's capacity to deal with ambiguity and complexities. According to his theory, at each level of development we make meaning in different ways and this leads to fairly predictable responses and reactions to authority, ambiguity, complexities, and self-responsibility. You might be asking yourself why this matters and what the relevance is for us as coaches and leaders. I'll provide a window into how this links to our work as I review the stages Kegan outlines, but for now, suffice it to say the world we live, lead, and coach in is more complex than ever before. The challenges we contend with are nuanced and ambiguous. Hence the popularization and relevance of the acronym VUCA (volatility, uncertainty, complexity, and ambiguity), the "new" crisis environment that makes the work of Self as Coach increasingly relevant.

Kegan describes the pathway to continual development as a dynamic "self-object" dance that provides a roadmap we can utilize to continually develop and transform the self over the course of the adult years. All that is "subject" is an unquestioned part of the self (rules, behaviors, beliefs, etc.). This subject drives us, is inside and thus invisible, and grows out of our awareness. All that is "object" is the opposite, because we can see it, control it, reflect upon it, and make choices relative to it. As we deepen our self through reflection and coaching, we continually turn subject into object, each time growing and developing a stronger sense of self. Kegan tracks the development of an adult through his model of the journey from the socialized self to the self-transforming mind (Figure 2.2).

Kegan views the path of our adult development through the lens of engaging in a continual self-object dance wherein we slowly shift

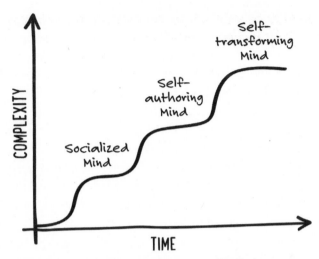

Figure 2.2 Kegan's Transformation of Self

our perspective from a state-restricted sense of self, largely dictated by external forces and norms, to an increasingly broadened and expanded sense of self where we attend to our own development in the face of evolving external and internal realities. In many ways, his work integrates the conceptual frameworks of attachment theory and Horney's work into the tasks and opportunities available for continued development in the adult years.

His concept of the self-object dance suggests we are essentially run by our self (our stories, stances, and scripts) until an event or series of events (external or internal) allows us to see the self and shift it to object to gain a view of the stories that metaphorically imprison us. When this occurs, the self becomes object and when our stories are object, we can separate from them, see them, and create some space between the story and our self. This gives us choice. At first the choice may be fleeting and limited, but with enough attention to the story, subject transforms into object and we experience a new layer of self, a new identity of sorts with new choices.

According to Kegan, in self mode, I am unable to see my stance, my story, my limiting beliefs, and my habits—I simply *am* my stance. When in object mode, I am able to step back and take a look at myself at a distance and I can start to separate myself from my stance. In this position, I have choices because I have developed the capacity to observe self, thus turning it into object, and this opens the door toward choice. As seen in Figure 2.3, Kegan refers to the early stage of development for the adult as the *socialized mind* and the progression from socialized mind to *self-transforming mind* requires conscious work on the self. Kegan speculates the percentage of people who reach the pinnacle of self-transformation is few.

At the socialized mind stage, there is a drive to follow rules, to largely understand the world through the views of sources external to self and to view issues and challenges as right/wrong, black/white. This person will easily take the viewpoints and perspectives of others (religions, companies, etc.) and view the world through this singular lens. Authority is found outside of this person and when a conflict occurs between their values and those of another, this individual feels a deep internal wrenching that is hard to bear because there is not a well-developed sense of what I want beyond the societal rules and expectations that have been introjected. Evolving from this stage requires the individual to step back (turning self into object) and notice this tendency repeatedly until the individual is able to move into a new layer of development and experience more of the greyness of issues and challenges in life. The socialized mind must find ways of anchoring one's self (and thus move more toward the self-authoring mind) while considering external viewpoints, as well. This requires our consciousness, intention, and repetitive awareness over time. In the work setting, socialized minds need direction and approval to feel comfortable. In the work of coaching,

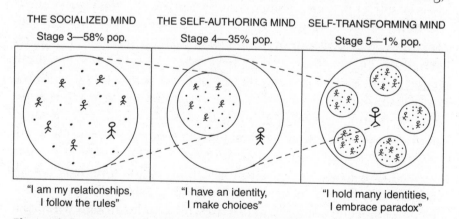

| THE SOCIALIZED MIND | THE SELF-AUTHORING MIND | SELF-TRANSFORMING MIND |
| Stage 3—58% pop. | Stage 4—35% pop. | Stage 5—1% pop. |

"I am my relationships, I follow the rules"   "I have an identity, I make choices"   "I hold many identities, I embrace paradox"

Figure 2.3 Kegan's Constructive Development Theory
Source: Adapted from *In Over Our Heads,* by Robert Kegan, 1994, Cambridge: Harvard University Press.

coaches who do not move past the socialized mind likely look for the right tools and the right next steps in the hopes that it will ensure the success of the engagement.

Leaping into One's Own Set of Rules

Those who reach the *self-authoring* stage have internalized their own set of rules and beliefs and they use their internal rudder to make decisions. They are able to experience empathy for others when their views differ, but unlike the socialized mind, they don't feel torn apart by the inevitable conflicts as they arise because they possess their own internal capacity to make decisions and develop perspectives. In the work setting, these people are self-directed and self-motivated. They own their work and likely don't flourish when a supervisor wants to micromanage them. In the work setting, those at this stage are equipped to evaluate themselves fairly accurately instead of seeking the approval of authorities in order to determine how they are doing. In the work of coaching, these coaches are more confident about exploring nuances, seeing realities different from their own, and managing their own judgments when working with the client.

Seeing Many Layers

The *self-transforming* stage where, according to Kegan, few of us reside is seldom reached before midlife and, even then, only occasionally attained. Those at this level are capable of seeing many layers and perspectives to every issue presented. At this stage, there is a capacity to hold conflicting perspectives simultaneously. Black and white doesn't exist and gray is everywhere. These leaders are not likely to be surprised by a crisis or an unexpected event because of their capacity to examine all angles of a situation. In the work setting, those at this level of development are sought-after leaders in a world that is vastly more complex than ever before. In the work of coaching, these coaches bring a depth of value to the work because they are not limited by their own beliefs, thus allowing spaciousness to explore a broadened landscape of possibilities with their client.

Kegan in Coaching Engagements

Kegan's focus on turning subject into object in order to continually evolve as adults has multiple implications for us as coaches. Research in the field of coaching has suggested that we can't effectively coach clients who are further evolved than we are. As coaches, it then becomes paramount that we have a view into our own level of development and a more granular ability to experiment with continually turning subject into object in our lives.

Matching Levels of Development of Coach and Leader

An interesting implication of Kegan's work has been postulated by Laske (2006a; 2006b) and supported by the work of Chandler and Kram (2005), suggesting that a coach will not be capable of adequately helping a client who is at a higher stage of development than their own. Laske writes "a coach who is at the same developmental stage as their coachee will not be able to help them get to the next stage, and a coach at a lower stage of development than their coachee may actually impair progress." Given we are subject to and restricted by our meaning-making capacity at each level, we view our meaning-making as "the way the world is," which makes it nearly impossible to consider other perspectives.

This perspective fortifies the need to emphasize the coach's focus on development of one's internal landscape. Inevitably, in this exploration a coach bumps into their meaning-making in ways that are positively challenging and encouraging of growth. Becoming a great coach capable of supporting a leader engaging in vertical development requires a fierce commitment to one's own ongoing development and continually cultivating one's internal landscape in order to be at one's best when providing great coaching to leaders.

The Granular Level of the Self-Object Dynamic in Coaching

I find it is possible to use this self-object dynamic at a granular level, as well. Take, for example, a coaching colleague who has spent years in a demanding high-level leadership role inside a fast-paced organization.

She comes to coaching with a kind of rat-a-tat-tat rhythm, a mixture of fast-paced intensity, kindness, and razor sharpness. This rhythm is invisible to her (it is subject) because she has lived it for so long and it has worked so well. While developing her coaching skills, she receives some early feedback about her rhythm and while open to the feedback, she is not sure it is accurate. A couple of months later she decides to ask her colleagues inside her organization (as she is about to depart the organization) for feedback on her style. Again, she receives feedback about the intensity of her presence and her rhythm. Now, with more input, she begins to consider this dynamic to be true (turning subject into object) and she becomes interested in understanding more about how and what she does in order to determine how she can start to adjust this long-held way of being.

Without this awareness, we have little choice but to live in our old stories and habits and, in effect, we are driven by our stories, limiting beliefs, habits, and ways of being.

Kegan's concept of this self-object dance provides a wide-angle lens into our own understanding of self as well as in our work with our clients. Neither coach nor client can change until we are able to step onto the balcony and gain new views of ourselves—our habits, stories and beliefs; nor can we as coaches change without these new views. Taking some liberties in translating Kegan's subject-object dance into more granular levels, Table 2.3 shows my examples of how a coach, or coach with client, might begin to make object out of subject.

To make object out of subject takes willingness combined with time and intentional attention. *Willingness* because first we need to want to gain new perspectives and make changes before anything can shift. *Time* because many of us spend decades developing our way of being and it takes time and discipline to create new pathways. *Intentional attention* is perhaps the hardest. We have to *stay awake* to what we want to shift—all of the time—and this is not the way our organism is built; even when life isn't working, we like to stay in our habits, routines, and old stories because we know them. There is comfort and ease in knowing and anxiety and fear of the new and not knowing.

Table 2.3   Making Object Out of Subject in Coaching Engagements

Well-Ingrained Behavior	Self	Object
Unapproachable	My stance may be one of keeping people at a bit of a distance because that was a safe strategy when growing up. Now it has become who I am and largely invisible to me. Even when people have provided feedback on this stance, I'm only vaguely aware of what they are observing.	Through extended self-observation and feedback, I'm able to begin to notice when I am creating distance, what I am doing to create the distance, what the cost is, and where the spaces are for new ways of being that invite people into my space with increasing ease.
Defensive	My stance may be one of routinely defending myself because that was a survival technique that seemed essential as a strategy when growing up. It is now a habitual way of being that hinders my communication even while I have little awareness of it.	Through in-depth self-observation and feedback, I'm able to begin to notice when I am in a defensive stance, what I'm doing to hold this stance, and where the spaces are for new ways of being that create an invitation for real discussion rather than the old habit of defensiveness that shuts down many chances for conversation.

Pleasing Others	My stance may be one of placing an over focus on pleasing others (often at the expense of pleasing myself) because pleasing others was the strategy that served me best when growing up.	Through concentrated self-observation and feedback, I'm able to begin to notice when I am leaning into the "pleasing others" space, what is triggering my impulse to lean in, what the cost is, and where the opportunities are to shift.
Moving to Action	My stance may be one of placing a high premium on moving to action because this was a strategy in my growing up that provided me with what I needed from my key relationships. It is now a habitual way of being that can hinder my communication and connection with others even while I have little awareness of it.	Through thorough self-observation and feedback, I'm able to begin to notice when I am leaning forward and moving to action, what is triggering my habitual response, what the cost of my action is in my relationships, and where the spaces are to practice leaning back and being.

OUT IN YOUR WORLD: RECOGNIZING THE SUBJECT-OBJECT DANCE

- What might be only vaguely in your awareness—subject—that you would benefit by shifting to object in order to strengthen your coaching?

- How might you uncover in yourself that which is mostly subject and driving you?

- Are there trusted colleagues or family members you could dialogue with to see what they observe more clearly than you are able?

- Give some consideration to well-ingrained behaviors in your work as a coach, and in your life, wherein you could experiment with the subject-object dance.

THE COACH'S WORKSHEET: DEVELOPING MORE RANGE

Visit www.selfascoach.com for an opportunity to step back and reflect on what meaning the work of Kegan has for you and what practices you might develop to keep honing your capacity as coach.

HORNEY, BOWLBY, AINSWORTH, AND KEGAN: UNCOVERING OUR STORIES AND STANCES

We can easily intertwine Horney's three positions with Bowlby and Ainsworth's work to see how our early attachments impact our stance in life as we develop and then overlay the subject-object work of Kegan in order to gain new insights into how our history has melded the stories and stances that have often become invisible to us—"the water we swim in" and the prisons that constrain us from being our full selves. In many ways, it is the work of Kegan that encourages us to acknowledge our early predispositions and then actively engage in exploring our internal landscape in order to expand our possibilities as human beings over the course of our lives.

If we are committed to being great coaches for the leaders we work with, identifying our stories, stances, and scripts is essential. When we start at home we are able to make this translation with ease when we work with our clients. We are able to step back and see the bigger themes and stories that fuel our client's circumstances and challenges.

OUT IN YOUR WORLD: CONNECTING HOME BASE TO LEVELS OF DEVELOPMENT

- Are there stories, words, or images that might represent you as coach at this time in your life?

- Might there be some way of integrating early attachments, stances, and your developmental path today?

- What newfound compassion might you have for yourself as a coach from reviewing these foundational concepts?

THE COACH'S WORKSHEET: DEVELOPING MORE RANGE

Visit www.selfascoach.com for an opportunity to step back from each chapter and reflect on what meaning it has for you and what practices you might develop to keep honing your capacity as coach.

THEORY TO PRACTICE VIA NICK PETRIE: VERTICAL AND HORIZONTAL PATHS IN LEADERSHIP COACHING

In a VUCA World, think Vertical!
—*Nick Petrie (2015)*

The writings of Nick Petrie highlight the distinctions between horizontal and vertical development in the life of a leader (and for our purposes, a great coach). His work provides a helpful link from Horney, Bowlby, and Kegan to the Self as Coach model, as he emphasizes the reality that vertical development requires deepening one's self-awareness in order to leap into a new level of maturity as a leader. In Figure 2.4, he juxtaposes vertical development with Kegan's levels of development and, in so doing, draws our attention to what is required for developmental coaching to occur wherein deep change and potential transformation may be an outcome.

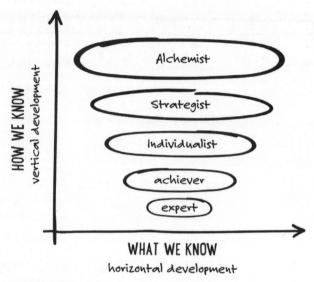

Figure 2.4 Petrie's Vertical Development

Petrie's work explores the distinctions between how we develop *horizontally*, wherein we cognitively take on new learning, technical skills, and abilities through reading, studying, memorizing, and putting to work the new skills we have acquired; and *vertically*, wherein more complex learning is the goal and it runs much deeper than taking on a new skill. In vertical development, the goal runs beneath the surface, requiring insight and unearthing of one's stories. It is in this coaching milieu that we transform who we are as leaders and human beings.

Going Deeper, Delving Vertically

This is the sort of developmental coaching leap that takes us to a new level of maturity in our way of being. Petrie emphasizes the need for vertical development as particularly important for leaders faced with the VUCA challenges of today's world. Consider the distinctions and synergy of both vertical and horizontal development in Table 2.4, and as you peruse it, you'll quickly see that we need both horizontal and vertical development. Yet, too often we are overly focused on horizontal development as sufficient when it is so often the case that it is disconnected from a leader's day-to-day challenges given the ambiguity of the VUCA context.

Table 2.4 We Need Both Horizontal and Vertical Development

Horizontal Development	Focus	Requirements
• Acquiring new knowledge • Developing new technical skills • Building new competencies	• Learning from an expert • Learning from the classroom • Learning from a mentor	• Experienced teacher able to transfer needed information • Experienced mentor-consultant equipped with ample tools and models
Vertical Development	**Focus**	**Requirements**
• Through self-examination that is potentially transformative, developing ability to lead in more strategic and complex ways when issues and challenges are complex and wicked.	• Self-awareness is essential in creating the opportunity for a new level of maturity to emerge.	• A seasoned leadership coach who has engaged in their own internal development and hence, is able to travel this terrain with their clients.

From My Inner Landscape: What I Learned from Petrie's Work

Cognitive learning, new knowledge, and skill acquisition are all important, but only when I am able to integrate these with deeper internal development that comes from plenty of heat, tough new situations, fierce motivation, and time for reflection and reorienting. I can read about the power of presence, I can believe full presence is important, but until I attend to what it requires for me to be fully present, it is just an intellectual concept.

Not so long ago I had a heat experience that grabbed my attention and took me deeper. A fellow colleague told me he sometimes experienced me as being distracted and not fully available when we sat down in my office to talk—an embarrassingly revelatory moment for me. This is not how I see myself and it is not how I want others to experience me. This is the domain of vertical development: getting clear on how I want to show up in important interactions with colleagues, building a self-awareness practice to tune into what ruptures my connection with another, and building actions to support full presence.

OUT IN YOUR WORLD: VERTICAL AND HORIZONTAL DEVELOPMENT EXPERIENCES

Using Petrie's distinction of horizontal and vertical development:

- Reflect on your learning journey as a coach and leader and identify those times you have taken on horizontal development and when you have experienced vertical development.

- Make a list and discern the difference in learning approaches and impact.

THE COACH'S WORKSHEET: DEVELOPING MORE RANGE

Visit www.selfascoach.com for an opportunity to step back from each chapter and reflect on what meaning it has for you and what practices you might develop to keep honing your capacity as coach.

FROM HERE TO COACHING LEADERS: A FEW FINAL THOUGHTS ABOUT THEORY

The roots of our development from the earliest years throughout the course of our adult years provide us with an enhanced perspective on being human. Our narratives and ever-evolving scripts become the prisons as well as the doors from which we view our world and live our lives. If our attachment is insecure or unpredictable, this early experience is etched into our psyche unless we actively seek to rework it; if our natural stance is one of stepping back based on early experiences, this, too, becomes a part of our fabric. As coaches, the depth of our work with leaders is magnified when we possess this more expansive perspective.

When we consider Kegan's levels of development through the early attachment lenses, it is easier to explore and examine what is at play for the leader who remains lodged in the socialized mindset, wanting to understand the rules, play by the rules, and hold others to that same playbook. This way of leading in today's world is not likely a successful approach and a tactical coaching approach that equips the leader with tools and techniques will likely do little more than put a bandage on a current situation.

A great coach is equipped to focus on a developmental approach that will supplement helpful tools and techniques (horizontal development) with a vertical approach to development uncovering the deeply held narratives and scripts, and providing a broader context beyond the current challenge or situation. Our ability to step back with a leader and gain the wider view of self, grow compassion for the roots of one's narratives and scripts, and allow the leader to see beyond a current situation and step into a change that is far more powerful and meaningful and translatable. This ability to fully grasp and incorporate the context of the whole person is what allows a coach to adeptly move between vertical and horizontal development in the service of what will serve the client.

How does a coach take the leap into one's vertical development, building a capacity to consciously move between horizontal and vertical dimensions with ease, capturing the best of both layers of development? Reading, memorizing good questions, building a great library of tools and techniques, possessing a practical methodology, building strong coaching contracts. Each of these is important and useful, but wholly insufficient to make the leap into the developmental domain of the vertical. The path to making this leap starts at home. As coaches, we need to engage in our own vertical development, we need to willingly explore our own stories and scripts and examine the roots in order to gain the broadened perspective that stokes the fire for our own development.

As Otto Laske (2006a, 2006b) found in his research, the coach cannot travel to places with their coachee that they, themselves, have not delved into. The coach cannot hold space for exploration of terrain that is outside their own spheres of discovery. So as coaches, we start at home.

Building on what we understand about how to support vertical development in the individual and knowing the sole purpose of this book is in support of coaches deepening their ability to use self as the most important tool in their work with clients, each subsequent chapter will explore how a coach can build practices for creating their own heat and how deepening these dimensions serves to create heat in our work with clients.

Chapter 3

BUILDING HEAT THROUGH CULTIVATION OF SELF AS COACH

> One can have no smaller or greater mastery
> than mastery of oneself.
>
> —*Leonardo da Vinci*

CULTIVATING SELF AS COACH BUILDS HEAT FOR THE WORK

Heat is a potent cauldron connecting head, heart, and gut in a mixture that creates an opening for meaningful breakthroughs—the sort that connect the dots, linking who we are today with our past, our narratives, our early attachments, and the scripts we crafted in our early years that no longer serve us as well in our current lives. Heat creates the possibility for new insights and epiphanies. With well-constructed practices and supports, these breakthroughs lead the way to our own vertical development.

Chapters 3 through 9 focus on the six dimensions of Self as Coach and include conceptual links to the foundational theories explored in Chapter 2. The following chapters examine how, as coaches, we can create heat through our use of self and provide practices to begin to incorporate new ways of being into our own sense of the self as a coach.

Figure 3.1   The Self as Coach Model

The six dimensions of Self as Coach are: Presence, Empathy, Range of Feelings, Boundaries and Systems, Embodiment, and Courage (see Figure 3.1). Our most worthy goal as a great coach is to remain at the edge of our growth, always feeling appreciative for where we find ourselves in our development, and simultaneously leaning into new layers and emerging opportunities to deepen our capacity as coach.

In this model, there is no arrival point and there is no perfection. Instead, great coaches share a willingness and a commitment to meeting one's self at the edge of the boundaries of one's development. Each of the six dimensions of the Self as Coach model appears as distinct but, in reality, we utilize various dimensions to different degrees and in overlapping ways with each leader with whom we work.

The greatest, and at times most enigmatic, tool that we possess as coaches is a well-developed internal landscape. This is our Self as Coach"—the whole, cultivated, managed self we bring to the coaching experience to inspire and help effect change. The cultivation of self explored in the following chapters is a never-ending unfolding that we owe to ourselves and to the client systems we serve in order to do our very best work with a developmental focus that ultimately changes who we are as human beings.

That said, Self as Coach is a challenging and sometimes elusive concept somewhere between reality and possibility. It embraces who we are, who we want to be, and who we need to be in order to be of true value to our clients. It requires us to be fiercely aware of our strengths, weaknesses, and tendencies. It demands that we call forth our talents, address ever-changing challenges, and constantly self-correct.

Understanding and using Self as Coach as the most important tool in our work allows us to move beyond simply using learned tools in the way an actor might play a role and to come to a place that models true development and supports the ability to change. Without use of our self as the most important tool in our work, we are wildly diminished, personally and professionally.

Without Self as Coach, we are left to wonder:

- What if our presence is so overpowering and dominating that a client is reluctant to share her real anxieties and concerns?
- What if our attachment to tools and resources and our tendency to lead with these diminishes our connection with the client?
- What if our tendency to emphasize the positive and veer away from the darker side makes it almost impossible for the client to explore what is most at stake – dark as it might be?
- What if our own raw edges make it difficult to slow down and build the all-important working alliance with our client?
- What if our own fears make us unwilling to help a client pursue a daring alternative?
- What if our own level of development is still in that early socialized stage of either/or thinking and we are unable to go with the client to where their focus needs to be?
- What if our aspirations are so strong that we fail to recognize that our client wants something much simpler, more direct, and more achievable, at least in the short term?

These haunting questions highlight the possibility that some elements in the self of a coach can either promote or undermine our clients' ability to achieve the changes they so richly desire and deserve. Of course, the list can be endless and you might even craft your own version, but the overriding message in these questions is that in order to do great work as coaches, we need to be thoroughly engaged in our own work with self at all times.

Early in the coaching journey, it's surprisingly easy to overlook the power of our own capacity (or lack thereof) and view the client as our challenge, perhaps resistant, unwilling to examine tough issues, or talking in circles. This attitude can make it difficult to bring the engagement to a successful conclusion. Yet, in most cases, the coach's own work on the inner terrain is what allows for something very different to occur during the coaching engagement. It takes courage and commitment for any coach to work the territory of self in order to engage at the highest levels.

Self as Coach work requires us to examine our own histories, our narratives and scripts, the natural limitations, the inevitable blind spots and rough edges in order to strengthen and extend our capacities. Delving into this dark woods is not for every coach, but if you are a coach willing to take this leap and are ready to engage in developmental work with clients that is enduring and often life changing, this is a path to being a great coach. At times tough and challenging, our heat experiences deepen us and enlarge our appetite for engaging in developmental coaching.

A COACH'S HEAT HELPS THE LEADER GROW

Fundamentally, a leader approaches coaching because there is something they want or need to tackle that is beyond their current capability, but still important in their leadership role and equally important for the stakeholders in their organization. The leader knocks on the coach's door when something in life is unsettled, unknown, in motion, or drifting away. Change naturally stirs anxiety and unease, and the nature of the relationship between the coach and leader is pivotal to the success of the engagement.

The leader's list of needs includes:

- A need to feel a strong sense of respect and unconditional positive regard.
- A need to experience a working alliance and sense of chemistry and partnership with the coach.

- A need to have a sense of partnering together instead of operating in a hierarchical arrangement.
- A fully engaged, committed, and present coach.
- A coach who has made our work a priority that will not get shuffled about or cancelled at the last minute.
- A coach adept and skillful in providing feedback, even when it isn't easy to receive.
- A coach willing to respectfully challenge the leader's thinking.
- A coach willing to share a perspective different than mine, perspectives the coach is not attached to persuading me about.
- A coach with a clear and transparent ethical compass.
- A clear contract that resonates and holds the leader accountable for reaching the finish line!

This is a formidable list for any coach! In order to attempt to meet these expectations and strive to engage at a masterful level, a coach needs to continually engage in learning about one's self from the inside-out: strengths, raw edges, fears, and aspirations alike. Organizational psychologist Ron Short (1998) writes succinctly about our human challenge in this regard: "Our biggest, yet least visible problem is that we think the world is outside of us, distinct and separate from us, this perspective is a simple human reflex." In order to operate from the inside out and develop a deeper inner dialogue, the coach needs to become very skilled at observing the inner states that drive their actions and responses.

THE POTENT COMBINATION: HEAT OF COACH + LEADER

Many of us come to coaching assuming it's all about acquiring tools and techniques to support our work, and instead we find that the most important tool is our self, and this requires a sincere willingness to explore the layers of one's inner landscape. The late master coach, Doug Silsbee, often said, "We do the work on our 'self' in order that we might be granted the privilege of working with our clients." This statement implies that the coach's work on self provides a deeper empathy and honoring of the challenges of a client given that the coach has authentically traveled similar roads.

So just how does a coach cultivate the Self as Coach domain in order to continually build capacity in their work with others? That is the focus of Chapters 4 through 9 of this book; each chapter will focus on one of the six elements of Self as Coach. I will describe the concept, explore the concept in case examples and stories, and end each chapter with practices for further development. As a coach, you might find it helpful to read one chapter, take a few notes, engage in some practices, and return to the next chapter in a few days in order to allow some time for your own reflections to emerge on this journey.

Matters of the Working Alliance

The field of psychology provides coaching with helpful foundational studies into what the essential ingredients are in a successful therapeutic relationship. While the work of coaching differs significantly from that of psychotherapy, both fields share in common the medium of the relationship and this provides us with useful parallels in understanding what's essential in the relationship between coach and client. In many ways, the Self as Coach dimensions serve to enhance or diminish the qualities of the relationship that strengthen the working alliance.

Bruce Wampold's studies (2001) on therapeutic outcomes find that the working alliance—the quality of the relationship between patient and therapist—is closely related to the success of therapy, especially when the client is asked to comment on the quality of the relationship. The key elements of this alliance include: the client's relationship with the therapist; the client's motivation to accomplish the work; the therapist's empathic capacities; and the client-therapist agreements around goals of the psychotherapy.

In distilling recent research on characteristics that impact the outcome of psychotherapy engagements, de Haan (2008) provides a list of variables that have a positive effect on psychotherapy outcomes, including:

- Empathy: de Haan includes respect, warmth, and authenticity
- Mental Health: meaning the therapist's own mental health

- Ability to Let Go: of your own values and embrace others' value systems
- Attractiveness: inspiring confidence and appearing competent

The research on the working alliance is particularly relevant for us in understanding the factors that have the most positive impact on coaching outcomes. What we learn from the field of psychology that is equally relevant in coaching is that the quality of the relationship—the working alliance—is vastly more important than any tools and techniques a coach might possess. Furthermore, there is a reciprocal relationship between working alliance and Self as Coach: The quality of this working alliance is dependent upon the self-awareness of the coach, and the Self as Coach model provides a closer look into the layers of self-awareness we can develop in order to cultivate a strong working alliance.

For each of the six dimensions, my approach is to not only define the dimension, but also to show it in practice—in both my own journey and in examples for how the practice might be undertaken in your journey as a coach. For those who are familiar with the Self as Coach concept from *The Completely Revised Handbook*, this approach is a deeper look at the dimensions introduced in that book, through the lens of how I have experienced it and with a new set of best practices for how you might approach each dimension in your work.

Chapter 4

PRESENCE

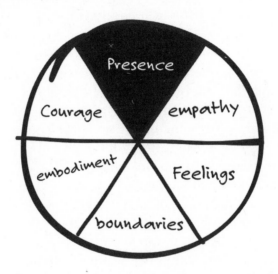

The ability to shift from reacting against the past to leaning into and presencing an emerging future is probably the single most important leadership capacity today. It is a capacity that is critical in situations of disruptive change, not only for institutions and systems, but also for teams and individuals.

—*C. Otto Scharmer (2013)*

GETTING PRESENT

To be a great coach, one committed to being fully awake and alert to ourselves and all that is around us, we need some sort of mindfulness practices. Practices that connect us to our internal experiences bring value to the way we relate, work, and coach. A practice builds our capacity to stay attuned to our self, center our self, and cultivate our internal dialogue in the service of doing our work well. As a wonderful friend and Buddhist chaplain, Claire Breeze, reminds us: "Mindfulness is not about sitting on a pillow; it's about building the capacity to tune into what is happening in the moment, to notice it and work with it. It's not about emptying one's mind; it's about noticing what's going on and building a practice of curiosity." A mindfulness practice, a discipline returned to daily, changes the way we relate, changes what we notice, and deepens our work as coach by cultivating our presence. Breeze also reminds us that it is impossible to get a mindfulness practice wrong. Find what works best for you, no need for crossed legs on a mat in a quiet room with a candle burning. There is no one right way!

While it's rarely useful to be prescriptive about the necessity of a practice, I am certain after many years of this work that we all need practices that continually cultivate our presence, support us, and become disciplines we can come to rely upon each and every day. Our deep presence is a cornerstone of masterful coaching work and there is no shortcut to developing our presence.

Life brings many lessons to us and over many years I have learned about the necessity and power of presence in times that are both joyful and painful—a well-cultivated presence changes the way we coach and the way we live in relationship to ourselves, others, and the larger world. Like many others, I thrashed about for several years finding a practice I could land on and routinely rely upon. I tried group meditation, I tried setting myself up with a mat in a specific spot for a daily meditation, I explored a regular walking meditation and, in the end, I realized I could create something unique that works for me.

Good Morning, Sun

Today, my favorite practice includes an early morning routine I like to call "Good Morning, Sun." I naturally awaken early before the sun has risen, I go downstairs, make myself a cup of coffee and then go back upstairs where I have a chair that looks out on a deep canyon with a view of the sun as it rises over the Pacific Ocean. I say good morning to the sun and I engage in my own personalized form of meditation. Sometimes I take only a few minutes and other times I allow longer periods of time to drink in the sunrise, appreciate all that's good and right in our world and then center myself for what is ahead for myself in the day. When I'm on the road I do my best to find a way to say good morning to the sun and often, in a city, it is an early morning walk as the sun is rising and the city is mostly asleep—magical! We live in a complicated world that doesn't always make sense, we do work that when done well, requires our full, undivided attention and we are often managing substantial workloads and commitments. For me, consciously creating space in the early morning to center myself, clear my mind and body, and notice what is showing up in me—this is a practice that I have come to rely on to be at my best each day.

Neuroscience provides ample evidence of the power of a mindfulness practice. Studies reveal that attention changes the brain and mindfulness strengthens our attention. Mindfulness is the act of simply noticing. As coach Claire Breeze reminds us, mindfulness is the "avatar of not knowing." Contemporary mindfulness practitioners reassure us we can make this work in our lives wherever we are and under any circumstances that work for us. This is a potent tool for deepening our presence and cultivating our continual development.

DEEPENING YOUR IMPACT: BUILDING YOUR DAILY MINDFULNESS

Practices

- Three Cleansing Belly Breaths: This takes only a minute, it is possible to do in the midst of a meeting or coaching session without others even noticing, and if used regularly it becomes a reliable support.

- The Lion's Breath: This takes a bit of space and privacy and can also be done in a minute or two, giving loud and deep voice to three or four big exhales.

- Individualized Presence Practices: These are often best when we customize what will serve us best. The secret is not in the *what* but in the regular discipline, the daily commitment to the practice.

A mindfulness practice builds our "curiosity muscle" and helps us to slow down to notice what is happening in the moment so we might use it well. We've all had moments when we deeply connect with another human being. Something almost magical happens for a few minutes, maybe a bit longer, and the essence of the connection lies squarely in the full presence of both humans in the conversation. For most of us, this is not an everyday experience, especially in our fast-paced world of today. So often we are on some wild triple-duty path attempting to engage in a conversation while texting someone and simultaneously considering another burning issue. This has become so common many of us find ourselves thrown off a bit when a connection happens that has this powerful quality of deep presence.

MY INTERNAL LANDSCAPE: WHAT I'VE LEARNED FROM DEEP PRESENCE

I mentioned earlier in the introductory remarks that I was married for many years to a brilliant man, great partner, and loving father of our three sons who was diagnosed with Alzheimer's at a relatively early age. The journey we went on together spanned several years and the nature of our connection continually eroded as his memory receded. Throughout the journey he taught me so many lessons about the power of deep presence. Early on in the disease, this required the simple act of slowing down (slowing *way* down) and matching his pace so we could connect in small conversations that were meaningful, sometimes fun, and always human.

The act of slowing down did not come naturally or easily to me. It took a lot of false starts and frustration before I began to notice that slowing required me to suspend old experiences of us and let go of how we used to be or how I wished our connection might be. As I began to develop my ability to suspend and let go, I noticed my presence grew and a stronger connection emerged—something fresh, unexpected, and much more real for both of us. Later, when he had very few words, he was present in ways that were harder for me to connect to. I was aware, though, that he was almost always acutely present to the sound of my voice. He couldn't reliably identify who I was in his life, but my voice signaled a safe harbor for him. Once again, when I could suspend what had worked in the past to connect, letting go of my desire for even the smallest of conversations, and deepening my presence enough to do this, I stumbled onto a profoundly satisfying way for us to be present for one another in a new form. He was a writer, reader, and lover of poetry. I knew all of his favorites and I turned to reading him some of his favorite poetry over and over each evening, suspending my old wish that he would speak and letting go of wanting to connect as we once had.

What unfolded was numinous. He would beam with joy, the anxiousness of his brain's state would recede for a time, and we would connect, present to one another in that moment and in that way. This was a daily practice for me for most of the last months of his life. I would hold a goal of consciously shedding work and demands of the day and intentionally turn my focus to be fully present to this precious relationship. Of course, I was imperfect and especially imperfect when I was in a state of *looking for* what I wished for: what had been, what I knew. When I could let go of the seeking and allow what *was* to simply emerge, I could begin to experience the power of deep presence, the work and discipline it demands, and the grace it creates in the human relationships that matter to us. While this experience is particularly personal and poignant, it easily translates to our presence in coaching—our ability to suspend, to be, to wait for the other to signal us through their offers.

THE WISDOM OF DOROTHY SIMINOVITCH

Dorothy Siminovitch, longtime colleague, master coach, teacher of a much-esteemed coaching program in Turkey, as well as a psychologist steeped in Gestalt, radiates and embodies presence like no one else I know. Maybe she was partially born with this gift and likely her years of immersion in the field of Gestalt therapy deepened this capacity. The field of Gestalt psychology focuses attention on the quality of our contact with another, examining how we extend, invite, withhold, or intrude into the space of another.

Siminovitch (2017) aptly reminds us as coaches, "our presence is an intervention." Powerful words, potent reality. Our presence is perhaps the most essential tool in our coaching quiver and presence (in whatever condition it might be) comes with us, shows up, and gets noticed the moment we have our first contact with our client, regardless of our awareness of self. Dorothy embodies her work in presence. It doesn't matter if we are sitting over a meal together, talking on the phone, or having an email conversation; her presence is palpable and the sense of connectedness I have upon ending our conversation buoys me. Something has changed. I have felt fully seen in this electrifying moment.

How do we pull apart the many strands that make up this deep and full presence, enabling us to come to our work prepared, grounded, breathing, alert, attuned to self, and attuned to our client? This rarified territory of deep presence requires preparation. It demands an ability to put the rest of life "on the shelf." It calls us into a deeper state of being that is intentional, grounded in all of the self and ready to do the work of coaching. This state we call *presence* represents our ability to be so thoroughly in the moment that we almost create a sensation that time has slowed down and, in so doing, a psychological broadening of perspective has unfolded.

IS YOUR PRESENCE AN INTERVENTION?

This is the work we must do to be at our best as coach. The task can sound daunting at first. While artificial, I find it helpful to pull apart the strands of presence and imagine there are actually layers of presence in ourselves, in our relationships with others, and in our surroundings, and when these three layers are in synch we are able to achieve this state of deep presence.

Figure 4.1 represents my observation over years of working with coaches, writing about coaching, and extrapolating from my own experiences as a coach. There are at least three dominant layers to presence that are helpful in our work: (1) presence to the inner rumblings; (2) presence to the relationship; and (3) presence to the ecology.

physical surrounding

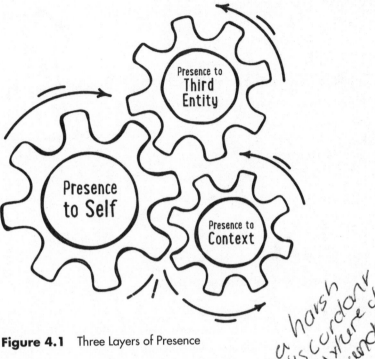

Figure 4.1 Three Layers of Presence

a harsh discordant mixture of sounds

PRESENCE TO THE INNER RUMBLINGS

Our foundation always starts at home. This is the essential building block (and thus the largest in Figure 4.1) that extends our presence in the other two domains, as well. Building presence to our own inner rumblings requires practices that allow us to continually draw inward with ease and cultivate awareness of our voices, our preferences, and the cacophony of our inner rumblings. The ability to journey inward and pay attention to my heartbeat, my pulse, my thoughts, assumptions, biases, desires, and judgments only comes with regular practice. We return to this notion of a discipline as essential for a great coach. Cultivating mindfulness supports our presence and ultimately requires a practice—one uniquely suited to you, not a prescribed practice you've read about. A disciplined practice allows us to be awake to what happens internally when we are not fully present. We cannot develop and sustain this deep presence without a personally customized, regular mindfulness routine that brings us closer to our self, allows us to notice the endless stream of internal chatter, and cultivates our capacity to center in the moment.

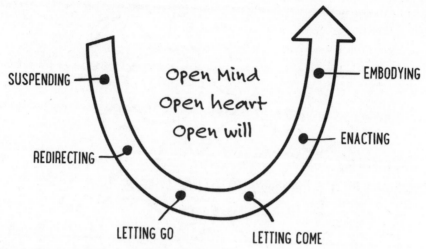

SUSPENDING

Open Mind
Open heart
Open will

EMBODYING

REDIRECTING

ENACTING

LETTING GO   LETTING COME

Figure 4.2   Scharmer's Theory U Model
Source: Adapted from Scharmer (2018).

For most of us, the common cast of internal characters impeding our presence is predictable; it includes our preferential minds: our judgment and biases, old stories, beliefs, preoccupation with something that is capturing our attention, and our incessant inner chatter. Sometimes these internal rumblings and intrusions are only vaguely in our awareness and at other times we are awake enough to our internal landscape that we can make adjustments.

Presence to our biases and assumptions is elusive and only vaguely on the periphery of our awareness. Otto Sharmer's Theory U model (2018), as shown in Figure 4.2, examines the internal path we need to travel in order to *presence* ourselves.

At the top of the "U," he recommends building a small practice to hang any assumptions and biases out in front of oneself in order to create the space to notice our naturally preferential mind, to wake up to the beliefs we are holding, to provide the needed space to create awareness and in so doing, begin to release them a bit. Following his U curve downward in Figure 4.2, he suggests that once we have taken this first step in what he terms *presencing*, we are able to observe what's being said and what's happening with a mind that is widened and slightly more open, able to let go of old stories and biases that impede our presence. This letting go leads to our ability to sense more and connect with heart, thus arriving at the bottom of his U in a state of presencing, able to engage in a thoroughly present conversation.

The coaching vignette that follows spotlights the power our assumptions and biases have in disconnecting us from our clients. You'll see in this description the unfolding of Scharmer's presencing process.

VIGNETTE: THE INVISIBLE COST OF A COACH'S UNEXAMINED BIASES

Martin's boss encouraged him to seek coaching to hone his leadership style. Martin is an older physician leader who is able to build a trusting and caring rapport with his patients; yet those who report to and work with him experience his leadership style as intimidating and on the verge of bullying. The head of his department asked him to engage in some coaching around this issue and while Martin was a little reluctant and felt he was in the last lap of his career, he was willing to step forward to explore.

If the coach fails to take the time needed to get present to any assumptions or biases that might arise based on a brief conversation with Martin's boss and Martin himself, the coach's full presence would likely be impeded. Without taking this moment, a coach could easily walk into the first session aware that they find his bullying behavior particularly noxious and they could also be wondering if at his age he will be interested, willing, or able to make any changes to this behavior. If the coach proceeds without bringing these assumptions and prejudices, which include old experiences and unexamined ageism biases, into full awareness, they will compromise presence, alter their approach, limit the ability to create a strong working alliance with the client, and generally degrade the quality of work that can be done together.

Sometimes building presence seems like it ought to be easy and simply focused on managing ourselves as coaches. The simple stuff of schedules, pace, attention to space—it turns out not to be so simple and makes a big difference in how our work unfolds. This vignette tracks the impact of unmanaged preoccupations!

VIGNETTE: WHEN PREOCCUPATIONS SUBVERT OUR ATTENTION

Yikes, My Clock Is Running Me, Says the Coach: Regrettably, we've all been there from time to time when our presence is not optimal. The story is familiar to most of us. The day has been busy, we didn't take enough time to review the calendar the night before, the morning started very early, and then it happens—two or three minutes between appointments and the next one is a coaching call. Without sufficient time to review notes or the space to get one's self fully present, we walk into a coaching session feeling uncentered and wobbly. The toll this takes on the coaching session that ensues is undeniably significant. When a coach hasn't taken the time to get present to self or pay attention to the themes of their coaching work, they are left entering a coaching session focused on calming the self in the moment, madly working to put on the shelf any leftover emotions from the last call they were on. Now, the coach's inattention becomes a part of the coach-client third entity impacting what can be accomplished in this session. We all get it; nobody wants to be in this compromised position. Yet, I often have coaches tell me there is no choice and no time to create space to get present. The list of reasons, which sounds on the surface rational and reasonable, is long. The reality is, in this all-important presence domain, this is the simplest level of presence we can attend to. It requires us to set our intentions and create clear boundaries and then, live by them. In the world most of us are living in, this takes a heavy dose of self-management and transparency, allowing us to stay truer to ourselves, to take our recovery as seriously as we take our work states, and to build practices that support this discipline of full presence.

DEEPENING YOUR IMPACT: CULTIVATING FULL PRESENCE

- Build a 30-day practice using a notepad twice a day to simply record any awareness you had throughout the day of biases and assumptions about others. Jot short notes, keep it simple, and on Day 30, see what themes you can learn from!

- Practice *more asking* and *less assuming* by equipping yourself with some simple inquiries that may potentially alter your perceptions. Questions such as: *Do I have this right?*, *Is this what you mean?*, and *Are you saying … ?*

- Regularly disrupt your opinions and beliefs by asking yourself, *Is that really so?*

Another dimension of our inner rumblings is the constant chatter roaming through our minds, this cast of characters inside our heads that gets in the way of our full presence. Some common chatter you might recognize:

- What should I ask next?
- What is the best solution?
- Haven't I experienced something similar to this?
- Am I doing the right thing?
- Am I failing my client?
- What time is my dinner meeting tonight?
- Oh, I am feeling tired!
- Why is my client talking so much?

Without a mindfulness discipline and a focus on our full presence, we go off track routinely through our conversations, our coaching, and in our most important interactions. Our version of off track might be subtle and almost imperceptible, but it turns out in coaching—work that is highly relational—the impact is significant. Years ago, I spent time training in Gestalt Therapy with Miriam and Erving Polster, early founders of Gestalt following in the footsteps of Fritz Perls, in the late 1970s. In our group work with them they would speak of the "resonance chamber" we create with another when the chatter is at bay and we are fully centered and in the moment with the client. They would constantly observe when we left that resonance chamber. Calling attention to it heightened our awareness of the degradation of our presence and the loss of connection with the other when the chatter was front and center.

DEEPENING YOUR IMPACT: STRENGTHENING YOUR RESONANCE CHAMBER

- Take two weeks and following each of your coaching sessions, track those times in a session when you were fully present. What were you doing, what were you being that allowed for that full presence? Take notes and see what you can uncover that is helpful going forward.
- Pay attention as well to somatic cues *relating to the body* when you are in this resonant state to see if you are able to identify some signals that support your resonance.

Finally, our inner rumblings also track, albeit sometimes vaguely, the innumerable stressful situations that have occurred throughout our days. In today's world, the variety of common stressors continues to grow: freeway traffic, endless email activity, longer work hours, travel delays and snags, conflicts, and disagreements at work. If you have an active family, these stresses likely grow exponentially. Many suggest we experience at least a dozen of these stress events on a daily basis. This is normal for all of us; yet our capacity to track and manage our stresses can impact our work. If you are feeling stressed and out of sorts, this will inevitably hamper a strong resonance with your client.

According to current neuroscience research, our inevitable daily stress occurrences set in motion a series of hormonal reactions beginning with the secretion of epinephrine and norepinephrine into our bloodstream. These secretions raise our blood pressure and our breathing becomes quicker and shallower. Simultaneously, the body begins

Study of the nervous system

to release cortisol into the bloodstream, rendering us cognitively and emotionally impaired. In other words, a stress situation sets in motion a complex internal hormonal reaction.

If, as coach, you are not adequately present and awake to notice and attend to this stress reaction, this will impinge on the resonance you are able to create with your client. Without an awareness and attunement to our stress levels and without an adequate practice to bring ourselves back to center, our presence is considerably diminished.

In order to be responsible as a coach, we need routine renewal moments in our life spread throughout the day. What qualifies as a renewal moment or a renewal practice? Well, many of us might label the end of day glass of wine, a weekend nap, or a summer vacation as our reliable renewal practice, but none of these is sufficient. Our renewal practices can't be accomplished in a single vacation or long nap. They need to be fully integrated into our daily routines. As Boyatzis reminds us, we can't effectively engage in "binge renewal." Instead it must be fully blended into daily life, allowing us to call upon these practices when we need them. The space between a stress event and our ability to return to center is when we need one of these practices most.

DEEPENING YOUR IMPACT: STAYING FRESH—A RENEWAL PRACTICE CHECKLIST

- Create music playlists for renewal and have these readily accessible in the office, at home, in your car, and when walking.

- Find a reliably soothing walking path that is short and easily accessible for a short renewal walk.

- Keep a favorite book of poetry or two nearby with *quieting* choices earmarked.

- Invoke your mindfulness practice.

- Use a body-oriented practice like yoga, tai chi, aikido or your favorite to *unhook*.

PRESENCE TO THE RELATIONSHIP

Presence to our inner rumblings is the condition that allows us to fully turn attention to the relationship. Given our work in coaching happens in this field of presence, creating a strong resonance chamber allows for fostering of a strong working alliance. Only our full presence grants us the capacity to notice the whole client, including voice, language, message, emotion, body, and somatic signals—all the essential dimensions of our client. There is my domain, the unique domain of my client, and a third domain created when coach and coachee come together. Presence to the relationship with the coachee is our attunement to this third domain.

Our *We-Q*

Fridjhon and Fuller (2013) use the term *holonic shift* to describe this pivot wherein we shift our focus from solely the client in the room toward the unique domain of coach and client: a shift from EQ to Social Intelligence wherein we focus on the *we* or, as Peter Hawkins terms this, our *We-Q* (*Leadership Team Coaching*, 2017). Our awareness of the unique qualities and experience of this third domain provides valuable ground for exploration with the client. Attending to what uniquely emerges when you come together with this one specific client is a rich source of information for both of you.

What It Means to "Use What's in the Room"

When we are able to be present to the relationship, the "we-ness" of each coaching engagement, we can uncover possibilities for exploration that are easy to miss if we are focused on historical data. Irvin Yalom (2002), an early expert in group therapy and later in individual psychotherapy, uses the concept of immediacy. He writes, "Immediacy refers to the immediate events of the session, to what is happening here—in this relationship, in the in-betweenness—the space between me and you and now." Yalom stresses that the work happening in a session (coaching or psychotherapy) is a social microcosm if we use it. The client who comes to coaching because they need to develop more presence in their role, and while in the coaching session avoids eye contact, rarely initiates conversation, and waits until the coach speaks, is demonstrating how they show up in other settings and the coach's reaction is likely to mirror the reactions of others. When the coach is alert and able to use what's in the room, stepping back and noticing, inviting coach and client to reflect, something new occurs. This here and now experience in coaching seems to heighten emotions and this often facilitates a critical moment for the client (de Haan, 2008).

This use of immediacy or turning up the heat is often a major shift for a coach because we have few relationships in our lives where we step back and freely comment on what we observe, what patterns we see, and inquire about how our client experiences this. In the early stages of coaching, we need to remind ourselves this is a contractual relationship that is vastly different than a social relationship. Those seeking coaching want to make deliberate changes and this is a very different space than most others.

DEEPENING YOUR IMPACT: BUILDING AWARENESS OF THE "THIRD ENTITY"

Mentally scan your current clients and ask yourself some of these questions:

- What is the unique quality of our connection?
- What and how do I feel in the presence of this client?
- What can I learn from my own internal experience?
- What is my experience in relation to this client that is distinctive?

In the following vignette, a coach describes the dynamics of a client interaction that create a particularly unique situation relative to this "third domain."

Using What's in the Room: Cultivating the Third Entity

As you read this vignette, pay close attention to the third entity and see what you notice.

VIGNETTE

Raphael is coaching a client he is finding particularly challenging. His client is a senior leader in a demanding role and a fast-paced industry. The client typically takes their coaching call while either driving or being driven into his office in the heart of a large urban city. Raphael finds this dynamic distracting and challenging and he has an inclination to ask his client to change this distraction by only taking coaching calls from a private office. As he steps back and looks at this situation through the holonic lens or a We-Q perspective, he instead uses what is "in the room", sharing his experience of finding himself distracted during the calls as horns are honking and the occasional ambulance siren is zooming by, finding it hard to stay connected to the client around the coaching exploration. Raphael admits to his client that it is common for him to feel some anger rising during these calls, as well. He uses nonjudgmental language that provides the ground for exploration and comments, "We've been engaging in this coaching for a couple of months and what I notice is how hard it is for both of us to stay connected to what seems like an important topic as sirens and horns are sounding off in the background. Honestly, I'm aware that at times I lose my own concentration and even find myself a little annoyed at the spin all around us. I wonder how this works for you and what you notice? I'm also aware that you have a desire to build stronger presence with your team and I just wonder if we could take apart what happens for us and see what we learn and perhaps how it is interconnected."

If Raphael had simply asked the client to stop taking coaching calls while driving or being driven, he would have missed an opportunity to use what was happening between them, in their interaction in the moment, and in himself as the coach. Ultimately, he would have missed inviting the client to reflect on their shared experience and the impact the environment has on the relationship. In this case, one of the coaching goals was strengthening this leader's connection to his senior team, so the potential breakthrough moment may be doubly meaningful for this coaching work.

DEEPENING YOUR IMPACT: CULTIVATING ATTENTION TO THE THIRD ENTITY

- Experiment with a metaphor that describes the interaction you have with each of your clients. You'll be tempted to build a metaphor solely about your client, so stay alert and use a metaphor that aptly describes your dance together.

- Spend the next week or two paying attention to what qualities are present when you come together with others in your life, be it family, friends, store clerks, and build your awareness of this third entity more often.

PRESENCE TO OUR ECOLOGY

When I say *ecology,* I am talking about the most basic, root definition of the physical surroundings that shape us as organisms. Presence to our surroundings sounds so simple and obvious and yet it is more multilayered than just location. It may not be standard for many of us to be in a coaching conversation while driving in the midst of rush hour traffic, but there is an inescapable reality that in today's world we manage the glaringly obvious environmental factors like the clock, our devices, and the physical environment we consciously create to do this work. If our smartphone sits beside us, it reduces our presence to one another. If our physical surroundings are in the midst of a busy restaurant or in an open space of an office setting where someone might pop in, these factors will impede our work. Paying attention to setting up the conditions for us to do our best work, for both coach and client to be fully present, this is an important ingredient for success.

Another layer of presence to our ecology is in our attunement to the broader ecosystem in which we are working: the corporate culture, the country and its culture, and the broader world. Geopolitical forces seem to have the energy of tectonic plates today and if we ignore these, we loosen our presence to our clients. I recall being in London working when the Brexit vote came in and my client was in such disbelief we needed to stop and spend a few moments acknowledging her reaction to what was very much in the air. Similarly, I was on an early client call in the United States the morning after the 2016 U.S. presidential election and, again, attention to a multitude of emotions and reactions to this event was essential before any other work could come into focus. In both cases, attunement to these broader geopolitical systems was essential. The ecology present inside the organizations in which we coach reveals another layer that requires presence. Not long ago, I was working inside a large system in the midst of a significant merger. The team I was working with literally didn't know who among them would stay and who might go. The anxiety was real and palpable. To proceed as though this reality could be ignored can only happen when we are not present to this layer of our work.

Our ecology is most commonly focused on the larger systems we are working in as coach and as client: the team, the larger department, the organization and their mission, the culture of the company or specific parts of the company. The timbre of the financial services industry is quite different than health care; the world of manufacturing looks and feels vastly different than that of today's tech companies. We must be present to these realities.

Once again, it is easy to notice these layers of presence are intertwined and the presence to self is at the core. Without this layer firmly in place, it's easy to get wobbly in our presence to the third entity and wobbly in our attention to environmental factors whether at the global scale or at the scale of a particular division of an organization inside which we are coaching. Consider some of these questions as you reflect on your current coaching engagements:

- Are you alert to major changes, challenges, and tensions that are present at this time in the overall organization and in your client's particular division and team?
- Are you attuned to any geopolitical tensions that might be on your client's mind and potentially distracting?
- Are you aware of your client's larger world—family, commitments, challenges, and tensions?

physical surroundings (handwritten)

DEEPENING YOUR IMPACT: STRENGTHENING PRESENCE TO ECOLOGY

- *Our Surroundings Matter:* We surely know that looking at the inbox on our laptop does not support presence nor does trying to have an important conversation in a busy restaurant setting serve our work. Our surroundings matter, from photographs, lighting, quiet, privacy—cues that support our presence allow us to get centered. Pay attention to your surroundings and explore any ways you can make small adjustments that will support your best work.

- *The Context of the Coaching:* Each context has a different feel to it, whether they are tech companies, financial services, health-care organizations, or manufacturing. When working with a leader inside an organization, spend time learning about the culture, what's unique, and what their current headlines are that are important for you to factor into the work.

Chapter 5

EMPATHY

understand + share feelings of another

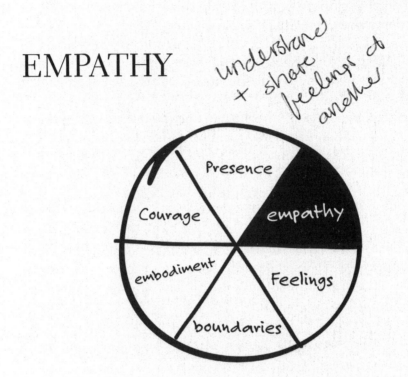

Self-absorption in all its forms kills empathy, let alone
compassion. When we focus on ourselves, our world contracts as our problems and preoccupations loom large.
But when we focus on others, our world expands.
Our own problems drift to the periphery of the mind and so
seem smaller, and we increase our capacity for connection—
or compassionate action.

—Daniel Goleman (2007)

The concept of empathy emerged in the twentieth century and is an adaptation of the German psychological term *einfuhlung*, meaning "feeling in." The definition of empathy began to change as psychologists began to study interpersonal dynamics. By the 1950s, psychologists began measuring interpersonal empathy in terms of connection. Edith Stein (1964) expanded the concept of connection by suggesting empathy is not simply confined to the connection to another's feelings or emotions, but is, in addition, where "the other is experienced as another being like oneself through an appreciation of similarity."

Today, consensus is still under study and the debate continues on the precise definition of empathy as well as the nuances of the concept. A growing, albeit controversial, body of research in neuroscience is engaged in research examining the role of mirror neurons—connections found throughout the brain—that allow us to mimic the action of others (Iacoboni, 2009), resulting in a convergence of emotional states that enable us to "feel" the emotions of another. According to Iacoboni, our mirror neurons aid us in reading another's facial expressions and, in so doing, feel the emotions of another. He argues that these mirroring moments are the basis of empathy. Figure 5.1 shows how mirror neurons travel from the insula to the limbic system.

I think of a recent experience I had with members of my family sitting and watching recent World Cup games. I have never played

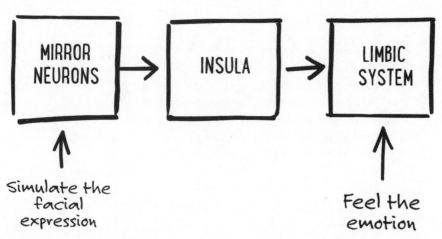

Figure 5.1 Mirror Neurons
Source: Iacoboni, M. (2009)

soccer and I don't understand all of the nuances of the game. I also had no connection to any of the teams that were playing. Yet, while I watched as one country reigned victorious over the other, and the pure joy and sense of euphoria appeared on the faces of those players, the coaches and the fans, I felt their joy and I teared up in the midst of their experience. My mirror neurons were at work!

The current studies of Iacoboni and fellow researchers suggest that mirror neurons provide an imitation of an observed facial expression and the neurons send signals through the insula to the limbic system, which seems to be the basis for empathy. The expanding research on the neuroscience of empathy continues to unfold and will undoubtedly continue to uncover new dimensions in our understanding of empathy.

We move between biology and psychology to fully understand the role and source of our empathic connections in our interactions. Social psychologist C. Daniel Batson (2009) has researched empathy for decades and argues that the term can now refer to eight different concepts:

1. Knowing another's thoughts and feelings
2. Imagining another's thoughts and feelings
3. Adopting the posture of another
4. Actually feeling as another does
5. Imagining how one would feel or think in another's place
6. Feeling distress at another's suffering
7. Feeling for another's suffering, sometimes called pity or compassion
8. Projecting oneself into another's situation

Karla McLaren's definition seems to distill Batson's work as she writes in *The Art of Empathy* (2013):

Empathy is a social and emotional skill that helps us feel and understand the emotions, circumstances, intentions, thoughts, and needs of others, such that we can offer sensitive, perceptive, and appropriate communication and support.

EMPATHY IN COACHING

Returning to Bowlby's work on early attachments, it turns out secure attachment early in life lays the groundwork for empathy. Those fortunate to have experienced loving, attentive parenting as children will access empathy with relative ease. As human beings, we find these moments where this empathic connection allows what needs to emerge to unfold if we allow it, if we are able to be present, if we can walk for just a bit in the other's shoes. As coaches, a strong empathic connection creates the working alliance that is essential in our work in order to engage in meaningful coaching. It is this empathy, this working alliance, that provides the coachee with a felt sense of being seen by another.

This concept of a working alliance has been written about and studied by many. Freud was perhaps addressing this when he wrote about "catching the drift of the client's unconscious." To be masterful coaches we need to know how to embrace and identify with our client's experiences, feelings, and the perspectives about their life situations they bring to the coaching. This is the essential ingredient required for coaching to be meaningful to the client. Kets de Vries (2014) writes that one's "empathic resonance is the process of understanding the other's subjective experience by sharing it vicariously, while simultaneously maintaining an observant stance." This empathic resonance paves the way for just enough safety to allow the conditions we need for breakthrough moments to occur in the coaching.

Creating Conditions for Breakthrough Moments

Memorable breakthrough moments in coaching don't just happen and we surely can't plan or force them; however, we can engage in our own work to enable the possibility for these moments. Cultivating the ground for breakthrough experiences requires a resonance factor, as thinking and talking alone is simply insufficient in accomplishing an important change. Empathy is the glue that makes this highly relational work of coaching possible. Without sufficient levels of empathy very little worthwhile work will occur in coaching. The client needs to feel connected and seen by the coach. The coach needs to feel equally connected and it is inside this relational field that meaningful works occurs.

We need to perpetually hone our ability to imagine what it would be like to walk in our client's shoes, to live in our client's experience. If we are able to do this sufficiently, our client feels seen and this sense of being seen creates a trust and connectedness that allows for our work to deepen. As a coach, we can express our empathy and our seeing the client in simple ways. It might be a few words like "Ahh, this sounds important," "I get it, this is big for you," or, with hand on heart, "This is hard." A few words express volumes to the client and provide that important sense of being seen by the coach.

Learning to Walk in the Life Shoes of Another

A few months ago, I had a call from a dear colleague reaching out to see if we could connect in the coming days as he had something important he wanted to talk about. It turned out he had just been diagnosed with a deteriorating condition typically accompanied by particularly challenging symptoms and simply wanted to connect. I had just seen him the previous month—vibrant, youthful, and healthy. He was a devoted father and had a demanding leadership role in a consulting organization when this distressing health challenge appeared at his door. The morning of the call, I was aware of how much I wanted to be there for him in a way that would be helpful and supportive. I knew this was not about taking action. I had no experience with this difficult diagnosis and I also knew the most important step for me was to take time to get fully present and centered for the call so he could have the very best of me.

We connected by phone and he shared some context, a bit about the business, his wife and children, his current state of well-being, and the complicated treatment plan. As our conversation meandered through all of this, he lightly mentioned that nighttime is the hardest. He finds himself restless and unable to sleep very well for it is at this time, alone in the dark, that the fears get magnified. His voice quivered when he spoke of the fears and we stayed here for a bit and gave voice to all that was heavy on his heart: the fear of not surviving, the fear of not being there for his family, the fear of not being able to

shared responsibility

successfully remain in the work he loved. It was a sacred moment—nothing to do, nothing to say, just the power of a deep connection that allowed him to give voice to these fears. For just a few moments we were together in that resonance chamber. We had no coaching contract, just a deep collegial connection and caring, yet this same attention to presence in the moment, to walking in another's shoes and to making space for what might emerge, is at play in all of our coaching work every day.

Empathic skills are accessible to all of us. Our empathy allows us to notice when a silence holds an important unspoken conversation, the meaning behind words and metaphors, or what's not being said. Empathic skills allow us to deeply connect with another. Neuroscience is now studying this empathic capacity that seems to reside in mirror neurons in the brain. Yet, as we explored in the work of Horney, Bowlby, and others, as children we learn very early that some emotions are not acceptable in our family or in a specific culture. As children we begin to categorize some emotions as positive and some as negative. As we mature, we don't have an acute awareness of those emotions that are worthy and those we shun, but as coaches who need to be able to empathize with a wide range of feelings and experiences, it becomes important to uncover for ourselves the go-to feelings solidly in our comfort zone and those that have largely been unconsciously off limits. This overlaps with the Range of Feelings dimension of Self as Coach, where we'll explore feeling in greater detail. For now, noticing our empathic connection is impacted by our access to feelings is helpful.

Empathy is multidimensional; it comes in different degrees and requires some calibration, for too much or too little impedes our work. Finding our resting spot on the empathy continuum (Figure 5.2) is important work for us as it helps inform where the edges of our development lie in this domain.

Imagine we could each place our general capacity for empathy on a continuum as shown in Figure 5.2. At the far-left side of the continuum one's empathy is nearly missing; in the center the calibration is well balanced; and on the far right one has an overabundance of empathy. We could likely link this to Horney's work and our comfort zone is likely impacted by our attachment style as outlined by Bowlby.

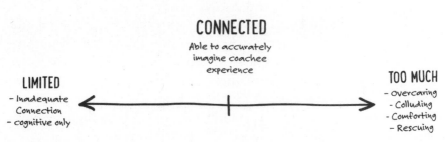

Figure 5.2 The Empathy Continuum

How do we locate our comfort zone on the empathy continuum, that spot where we find ourselves most often? Is it possible for me to become more agile? What does my resting spot enable and inhibit? Do I absorb others' feelings and find it hard to shake off a sad story a client shared? Am I prone to not noticing the emotional terrain of my client? These are important reflections for us as coaches, as sharpening our empathic connection is what allows us to create a working alliance to support developmental work.

Limited Empathy

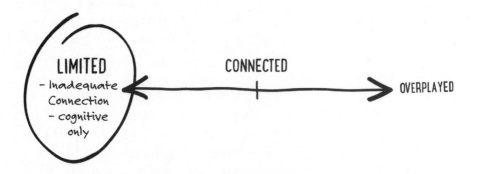

In Horney's terminology, if I am overly prone to Move Away, this will most often result in demonstrating too little empathy at the far-left side of this continuum. My ability to connect with the head, heart, and gut of my client is limited, perhaps because of my personal experiences and lack of full attunement to self. From this spot on the continuum it is likely that when a client expresses or shows emotions, the coach won't adequately attend to the emotions by noticing them and exploring their meaning for the client. The coach may simply miss the emotional cues and opportunities to provide their coachee with a visceral sense of being seen. Most often, this is where we reside when we are in our head and not present enough to ourselves or our coachee to notice our connection is very wobbly. Let's see how too little empathy can unfold in a coaching session.

Using What's in the Room: The Coach with Limited Empathy

Let's imagine a client, Anu, comes to a coaching session with an urgent issue that has just arisen in the past day or so. It's not a topic that has been on the coaching agenda, but it is front and center for her, with a sense of painful importance. In short, a surprise on the home front leaves her deeply concerned and close to tears as the session begins. As the coach you find yourself getting a little uncomfortable not knowing what emotions might come up and you might miss an opportunity to ask, "Would it be useful for us to put our coaching agenda on hold and spend a little time focused on what is happening for you right now?" Instead, you remind the client of the focus of the engagement and where the conversation was left at the end of the last session and, without referring back to the client's current distress, you suggest staying on course with the coaching goals. This is a missed moment to connect empathically with this client who is struggling and hurting about a situation that has just come up and is grabbing all of the client's focus. This sort of detachment from the emotional terrain is apt to create a disconnect, a sense from the client that he is not "seen" by the coach. We don't need to do much to create that empathic connection. It can be as simple as acknowledging the teariness or what sounds like a really tough spot, maybe an inquiry to see if the coachee would like to step back from the coaching focus and talk about it for a few minutes. Without this connection, the trusting resonance between coach and client is diminished and this lessens the likelihood the coaching will result in breakthrough moments that matter to the client.

Empathy Overplayed

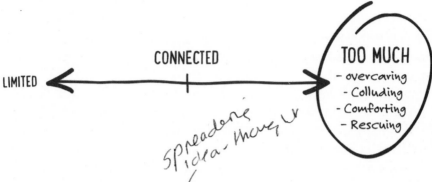

At the right of the continuum, we land in Horney's Move Toward territory that can result in too much empathy. McLaren (2013) terms this domain *empathy contagion*, wherein the coach is overwhelmed by the emotions and situation of the client and there is an experience of almost absorbing the client's feelings. The client cries, the coach wants to cry; the client is panicked, the coach feels panicked; the client has a strong sense of urgency and the coach adopts the same urgency. When feelings are expressed in the coaching session, the coach takes them in and when our empathy is over-calibrated we get drawn into our client's story rather than helping the client to see their story. Often a telltale sign of too much empathy is when a coach feels exhausted and wrung out at the end of a coaching session. Returning to our continuum for empathy, let's look at a vignette of when a coach is too far on the right-hand side of the spectrum of absorbing the coachee's emotions.

Using What's in the Room: The Coach with Empathy Overplayed

You've been coaching Mia for the past two months and your coaching focus has been on helping her strengthen her decision-making skills as well as her communication style with the team she leads. Progress has been slow, Mia's commitment to making these changes has wavered and you've been aware of how important this goal is for your client, her team and the goals of her unit in order to reach important targets. She arrives at the session today close to tears and announces that she has just received some shocking news that is very distressing. She tells you she has just learned her position is being eliminated. She is stunned. She is a single parent with two young kids she needs to support, she is in a panic and wants your help figuring out what to do and how to find another role for herself as quickly as possible. As coach, you feel awful for her and even wonder if there was something you could have done to help her avoid this situation. You immediately roll up your sleeves and let Mia know you are there for her. You have some connections you believe could be helpful to Mia and you are ready to come to her aid. You suggest another coaching session in a couple of days and a focus on polishing her resume and developing a plan. You find yourself worrying about Mia and wondering if an encouraging reach-out before your next session would be helpful as added support.

When we are overly empathic we become a sponge absorbing the client's experiences. Our first response to our client veers into the heroic over-functioning domain rather than a coaching approach. Too much empathy reliably leads a coach into the rescue mode and in so doing, the coach crosses the boundary into the client' story instead of helping the client see their story. Mia's situation is interesting. She had reliable information she needed to adjust her decision-making and communication styles yet she was slow to take any meaningful action. When her position is eliminated she is shocked and if a coach errs on the side of an overly empathic response that includes rescuing Mia, it will do little to help her uncover how she arrived at this tough spot and what she might learn as she moves forward.

WALKING IN A CLIENT'S SHOES WITHOUT WEARING THEM

The center portion of the continuum is when we are at our best as coaches. Noticing feelings and cues as they arise, honoring these with the client, and avoiding over-identifying and losing a coaching rudder that allows us to do our best work. Enough, but not too much. We are able to walk in the client's shoes without wearing them. We are fully capable of taking the client's perspective without losing our balance and boundaries. Gauging, regulating, and calibrating our empathic stance is fundamental in great coaching. Each of us has our own inclinations based on our histories and stories, and each of our clients elicits different responses and reactions in us. Somewhere in the mix of what we bring as coach and what we choose to respond to in our clients lies the balance of our empathic stance, allowing us to build a strong working alliance. Returning once more to the continuum for empathy, let's look at a vignette of when a coach strikes a balanced empathic response.

Using What's in the Room: The Coach Who Walks in a Client's Shoes without Wearing Them

Let's return to Anu's situation. She comes to a coaching session with an urgent issue that has just arisen in the past day or so. It's not a topic that has been on the coaching agenda, but it is front and center for her, with a sense of urgency. In short, a surprise on the home front leaves her deeply concerned and close to tears as the session begins. As the coach you immediately observe Anu's signals that she is not her usual self, that something is happening. You ask how she is and she quickly unleashes what has happened. As she does this you observe somatic signals and hear a quiver in her voice: She is upset and close to tears. Your hunch is that if Anu isn't able to talk about what's been happening, she will not be able to explore anything related to the coaching she is engaged in with you. You ask her, "Would it be useful to put our coaching agenda on hold for a bit and stay with what's going on for you right now?" She looks relieved and with tears running down her face, she laughs a bit and says *yes* and immediately reveals what is unfolding and what her worries and concerns are about all of it. You allow her to talk while you mostly listen and after a few minutes, Anu turns to you and says, "Thank you, that was so helpful to put words to all of it—I'm ready now to return to what we have been focusing on."

When we are able to strike a balance of just enough empathy there is a sense of being *in synch*, resonating with the client, making space for the client to think and feel for themselves. We are connected, we are aligned, and we are not enmeshed or rescuing the client. We are able to accurately identify emotions in ourselves and in our clients.

CALIBRATING AND CULTIVATING YOUR EMPATHY

Whether you find yourself needing to recalibrate and create stronger boundaries around your empathy so you don't wade into the rescuing territory or you are at the opposite end of the continuum needing to cultivate more empathy, there are plenty of ways to calibrate and cultivate.

One practice for cultivating empathy is figuratively sitting in the seat of your coachee or walking in their shoes by practicing seeing the world through their eyes instead of your own. Imagining their worldview and their responses to their situation with compassion.

Another practice focuses on the coach's self-care and resilience. It turns out there is a correlation between empathy for others and empathy for self. Engaging in self-care as a coach builds resilience, and it also seems that when we are attuned to what we require for ourselves to feel at our best, we are better equipped to notice what others need and this allows us to make stronger empathic connections. The old phrase "put on your own oxygen mask before helping others" seems to apply for us as coaches, as well. How do we attend to our own self-care as coaches?

DEEPENING YOUR IMPACT: STRENGTHENING EMPATHY REFLECTION AND SELF-CARE

Walking in the Shoes of Your Coachee

- Spend time imagining the coachee's situation from their perspective, not yours

- Spend time seeing the coachee's responses through their experiences, not yours

Building Your Empathy and Resilience Through Self-Care

- The basics matter—sleep, healthy diet, wellness routines.

- Time on the balcony: a regular practice of stepping out of being in your work as coach and looking at your work is a practice of self-observation that allows you to determine where you might recalibrate.

- Deliberately setting boundaries and managing any tendency to be a sponge for others' emotions.

- Finding your current version of best balance, including how many clients you are able to work with effectively and the nature of the engagements (travel time, intensity, duration, etc.).

- Building small practices that support your presence day-to-day. It may be creating a buffer between clients to take a short walk, doing some deep breathing, noticing what you need to put on the shelf to be at your best.

- Creating disciplined practices that cultivate being at your best—solitude time, walking rituals, yoga, meditation, journaling. A discipline is a commitment so the nature of what you do needs to work for you.

WIDE-ANGLE EMPATHY

break the law

And finally, another useful perspective on empathy arose not long ago when working with Peter Hawkins. Hawkins has contributed significantly to the body of knowledge in the coaching arena from supervision to team coaching to the broader context of change in our world; anyone in the field of coaching owes him a debt of gratitude for his body of work. One of the things I love about Peter is that he is a true provocateur prodding us, as coaches, to think in new ways. At one point in our time with Peter, he offhandedly added another dimension to empathy, which he terms *wide-angle empathy*, suggesting a coach is well served to practice empathy for all parts of the coaching engagement from the client in the room to all of their stakeholders, from direct reports to peers, boss, and the greater organization. He emphasized that a practice of broadening our empathy reduces tendencies to collude or rescue and encourages us to gain a perspective wider than the client in the room. This is a powerful and provocative challenge to coaches: How might our work be different and our perspective enriched if we were to engage in this wide-angle empathy?

strong reaction

GETTING OUT OF YOUR COMFORT ZONE: BUILDING RESILIENCE CREATES EMPATHY

Resilience is a requirement, not an option. To be great as coaches we need to engage in our own renewal practices; commit to taking good care of ourselves physically, mentally, and spiritually; and cultivate our agility. When we build resilience we also build empathy that extends beyond that which we have experienced or fully understand. There are all of the common ways most of us approach resilience—good rest, adequate unplugged time, mindfulness practices, breathing routines, exercise, and healthy diet. All of these ways of caring for ourselves matters. It is simply impossible for us to do our best work without these basics in place.

Another way we build resilience and agility is regularly disrupt ourselves. When we get out of our comfort zone, try something new, step into space that is largely unknown to us, we build resilience. It's at these times that we stretch ourselves and strengthen our nimbleness. Stepping into new spaces can be achieved in small ways and bold, from taking a class in an unfamiliar area, traveling solo to a new city, walking on a new path, or reading in a new genre. Resilience-building takes many forms.

Seeing the World Through Others' Eyes: Taking the Chicken

I have had the pleasure of working with a large social impact organization for several years. Teams are dispersed throughout East Africa with hubs in parts of Kenya, Uganda, Rwanda, Tanzania, and Zambia. Their mission is to enable farmers to increase the yield of their crops through better farming practices and higher quality seed and fertilizer. The organization provides loans to farmers to invest in these items and repayment occurs on a weekly basis. On a recent visit, I went out into the field to a farm setting where a weekly repayment meeting was about to occur. Farmers came from the surrounding area and each made payments of a size that was manageable for them. Unbeknownst to me, they were aware that I was joining in this meeting and, knowing I was an "elder," they wanted to honor me.

Honoring me turned out to be presenting me with one of their well-loved, egg-producing chickens (I mean handing it from one of the women directly into my arms). When I caught wind of what was to occur I immediately whispered to the field leader that this was not a good idea, reminding him they need their chickens to continue to produce eggs for them. Never mind that the thought of holding the chicken wasn't in my comfort zone! The team leader (much younger and wiser than I) whispered back that I must take the chicken, that for these farmers it would be an insult to refuse it. This was their way of honoring me.

A new and unexpected experience! I needed to take the chicken and change my view, see the world through their eyes. I slowly stepped forward, took the chicken in my arms and thanked them for their generosity. It turned out to be a profoundly moving afternoon, and if I had remained locked in to my view of the world and how things ought to occur, I would have missed a precious moment of connection; I would have missed understanding the nuances of a culture different from my old, familiar one.

We build resilience when we step out of our comfort zone. I find this happens regularly when I am traveling solo to new parts of the world, figuring out transportation systems, ordering food when the menu is in a language I'm unfamiliar with, paying attention to other ways of living and being in our world. Of course, this is not the only way to build resilience and spark agility. We each need to find ways to get out of our habits and rituals in order to enlarge our view of the world, and to create more resilience and nimbleness.

DEEPENING YOUR IMPACT: CULTIVATING RESILIENCE

- Practice walking in the shoes of another, immersing yourself in their circumstances for a bit. Imagine what it's like to be in their setting.

- Take nothing for granted and check your understanding of another's situation to make sure you aren't blurring their story with your interpretations or stories.

- Expose yourself to new situations in big and small ways as often as possible.

THE COACH'S WORKSHEET: DEVELOPING MORE RANGE

Visit www.selfascoach.com for an opportunity to step back from each chapter and reflect on what meaning it has for you and what practices you might develop to keep honing your capacity as coach.

APPLYING HEAT: CASE VIGNETTE I

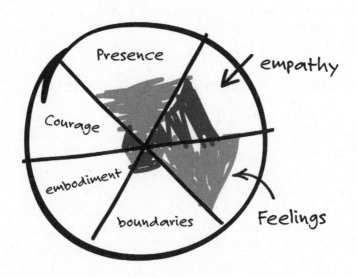

The three *Applying Heat* interchapters interspersed throughout this book provide case vignettes that synthesize common themes found in leadership coaching engagements. The purpose of these interchapters is to provide a real-time view of how the dimensions of Self as Coach translate into how a coach might approach an engagement, show up during the sessions, and use one's self on behalf of the coaching focus of a given engagement.

Following a brief vignette descriptor of a client situation are the reactions and perspectives of three different coaches and how their perspectives might be influenced or informed by aspects of the Self as Coach dimensions.

Naturally, the nuances of a real case cannot be fully captured in these vignettes. The purpose is to provide a glimpse into how the coach's ability to cultivate their internal terrain and enable the use of self supports both development work and the client's ability to make a change(s) that is important to them.

As you scan these interchapters, it's my hope you are able to see in practice what is being addressed in the six dimensions of Self as Coach. As you move through the dimensions, you may want to come back to the interchapters with fresh eyes on the coaches' responses.

CASE VIGNETTE #1: DRIVEN AND DISTRACTED

You've entered into a coaching engagement with a senior executive who, like most, has a demanding schedule and long work hours. In order to fit coaching into his day he needs the sessions to occur over his lunch hour tightly sandwiched in between other meetings. You've just finished the fourth coaching session and you are noticing it is very difficult to get a focus in the sessions because he is distracted by incoming calls that he feels are essential to take during the coaching sessions. You've never had this particular situation occur in your practice before and you are wondering how to deal with it.

Here's how three different coaches might approach this situation with the lens of each of the Self as Coach domains applied to enhance the applicability and relevance of the model.

Coach 1

Coach 1 is troubled by the distraction of incoming calls and kicking himself that he did not cover this territory carefully in the contracting, in the section on where and under what conditions can the best coaching occur. He believes his client sincerely wants to address some issues, but he notices how hard it is to get a focus for the work. He cares about this client, but is also aware of his own frustration and, at times, even annoyance at his client. He doesn't think it is smart to bring this dynamic up with the client and is worried that his client might be offended or think he, as coach, doesn't get how demanding his work load is. The coach wants to figure out what he could do to create a better way to approach the coaching, so they can get more focused.

Where Coach 1 Is in Each of the Six Dimensions

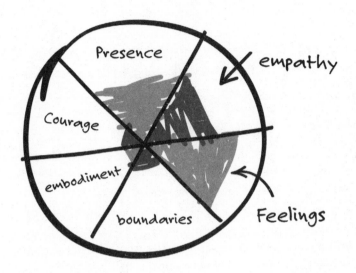

Presence. The coach possesses some awareness of his inner chatter and he has a bit of a sense of the we-ness that was created as they came together in this setting. He certainly has an awareness of the ecology because he mentions his concern about the circumstances of the setting and the tight scheduling that may not provide optimal conditions for coaching to occur. If he could amplify his inner chatter a bit more, he might be able to strengthen his presence.

Empathy. He shares that he cares about the client, so he seems to be developing a working alliance.

Range of Feelings. The coach seems able to contain the client's feelings, and has good awareness of his own feelings in the midst of the coaching sessions.

Boundaries and Systems. The coach worries about offending the client. This is his main reason for not sharing his own observations about the dynamics of their interaction. Offending the client and worrying that the client assumes the coach doesn't understand his heavy workload likely suggests the coach is getting drawn into the client's story instead of being able to *see* the story and use this information on behalf of the client.

Embodiment. The coach doesn't seem to be able to sufficiently center himself and connect to his somatic triggers in order to use them as cues.
Courage. Perhaps because the coach's boundaries are blurred, he finds himself wanting to please or certainly not offend the client, making it difficult for him to call upon his courage to share what he sees, what he experiences, what he observes, in a way that might serve their work.

Coach 2

Coach 2 is annoyed. She finds her own heart racing and rising as the calls come in and her client is engaged in providing rapid-fire input. She finds the situation untenable and disrespectful to her and their coaching work. She has never been in this situation before and kicks herself for not addressing the meeting place for the coaching during the contracting phase. At this point, she firmly believes the only option is to let her client know she is unwilling to work under these circumstances and bring the coaching to a conclusion.

Where Coach 2 Is in Each of the Six Dimensions

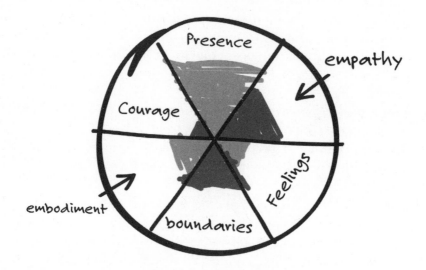

Presence. The coach appears so thrown by this client that she is not aware of her own inner chatter, or the we-ness of the relationship. She seems somewhat present to the ecology of the setting, as she has a heightened awareness of the setting as well as the tight space the coaching is being fit into: sandwiched in between other meetings.

Empathy. The coach seems thrown off by what is happening and her internal chatter is intense. These dynamics often create difficulty in fully connecting with the client and walking in his shoes for a moment. The chances are strong that the working alliance has not been well developed with him.

Range of Feelings. It's unclear how comfortable the coach is containing the client's strong feeling. However, she has good access to her own feelings.

Boundaries and Systems. The coach seems to be fully drawn into the client's story and her reactions are a part of her client's story rather than reflecting back on any useful or relevant patterns or observations.

Embodiment. The coach notices some somatic cues, in particular her heart racing, yet she is unable to use this as a cue or a trigger that could help her step back and re-center herself.

Courage. It may, on the surface, seem courageous to bring the coaching to an end, but it seems to be more of a defensive reaction rather than a courageous sharing of an observation or a perspective that might be useful to the client.

Coach 3

Coach 3 has never found herself in this situation before and takes some time to deliberately step back and make sense out of it. In the midst of the last two sessions she was aware of her own heart rate picking up and some anger rising in herself. When she stepped back for a bit and reflected, she began wondering how this same dynamic—rushed, not present, and unable to focus—might parallel how this leader shows up with his senior team and those working near him. She believes she has enough of a connection with her client that she can share with him the impact the situation has on her, all the while inviting her client to notice and consider how this might impact their ability to do good work. She also wants to explore where else this driven and energized presence might show up in his work. She isn't sure where this exploration might go, but feels it's important to bring up and test out potential parallels and then together find a path forward.

Where Coach 3 Is in Each of the Six Dimensions

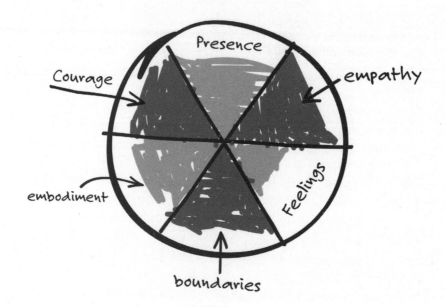

Presence. The coach seems attuned to her inner chatter, the we-ness factor, and the ecology of the setting. This presence will likely allow her to observe and see more in their work together.

Empathy. The coach reflects on her working alliance and seems confident she has a good sense of it and deems it to be strong. This is the essential connectedness that allows a coach to do their best work.

Range of Feelings. The coach seems able to contain her client's feelings and acknowledge her own. This ease with feelings allows a coach to travel wherever the client needs to go in the work.

Boundaries and Systems. The coach is able to step back and reflect, avoiding the tendency to get drawn into the client's stories. Her boundaries make it possible for her to see or at least explore together with the client what useful patterns show up when sharing observations.

Embodiment. The coach is tracking her somatic cues (heart rate quickening, face and neck heating up, blood pressure rising, voice changing, etc.) and she seems able to use these cues to help re-center herself when needed. This becomes a powerful tool for a coach both in preparation for a coaching session and throughout the session.

Courage. The coach has cultivated courage and upon reflection she has created a path forward to share her observations and curiosity about other parallels they might explore. This coach's ability to use courage (with heart!), share observations, and notice that which the client is only able to see dimly makes the coaching powerful grounds for vertical development and lasting change.

Chapter 6

RANGE OF FEELINGS

This being human is a guest house.
Every morning a new arrival.
A joy, a depression, a meanness,
some momentary awareness comes
as an unexpected visitor.
Welcome and entertain them all!
Even if they are a crowd of sorrows,
who violently sweep your house
empty of its furniture,
still, treat each guest honorably.
He may be clearing you out
for some new delight.

> The dark thought, the shame, the malice.
> meet them at the door laughing and invite them in.
> Be grateful for whatever comes.
> because each has been sent
> as a guide from beyond.
>
> —*Jellaludin Rumi*

When exploring the terrain of feelings, it is useful to address the distinction between emotions and feelings. They are essentially the same side of a coin with feelings arising from emotions. An emotion is a physiological experience that provides us with data about our world while the feeling is our conscious awareness of the emotion. McLaren's work on empathy and feelings provides a helpful pathway from empathy to feelings. As shown in Figure 6.1, first an emotion arises, we feel it viscerally, allowing us to name it, and finally, we act upon it.

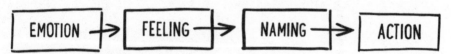

Figure 6.1   Pathway from Emotion to Action

Our capacity to track physiological cues of an emotion brings a feeling into our conscious awareness, allowing us to name the feeling and, finally, making choices about how we want to act on it or proceed. This path from emotion to action requires mindful attention that we hone over time. When we are caught off-guard and unaware of our physiological cues, we can find ourselves driven by, or even getting hijacked by, a feeling like flying off the handle or losing our cool. When we are able to pay attention to physiological cues like rapid heartbeat, rising blood pressure, warming of the face and neck, we are able to make choices.

What does a range of feelings imply? It is based on the reality that each of us has access to varying ranges of feelings. Another continuum is shown in Figure 6.2. On the far left, there is little to no access to one's feelings; on the far right, there is a rich and varied access that acknowledges variations in depth, intensity, and overlapping of feelings. Likely, most of us are somewhere in between these poles.

Let's walk along the continuum and you might start to locate yourself somewhere on it. You might also consider where some of your coachees are on this continuum.

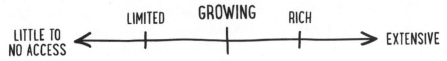

Figure 6.2 Range of Feelings Continuum

Little to No Access to Feelings

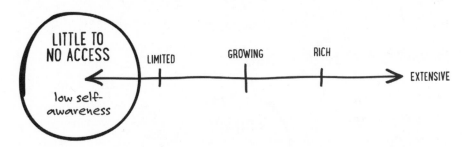

The psychological term for this is *alexithymia*, from Greek origins meaning *a-lex* (no words) and *thymia* (feelings). The term indicates an inability to describe emotional states. The person at this place on the continuum likely has very low self-awareness along with unique challenges in interpersonal connections.

A coach at this spot on the continuum will find it difficult to connect with a coachee enough to form that all-important working alliance because with marginal access to feelings it is harder to notice any feelings in the coachee, as well. In reality, it is very difficult to coach effectively from this spot because a coach needs to imagine the feelings of a coachee to create a strong connection as well as notice feelings as they arise in the coaching. Real change requires a combination of thinking and feeling in our work.

Limited Access to Feelings

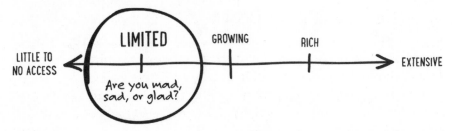

The repertoire is small. It may be the three states that are often referenced as mad, sad, or glad. A coach at this spot on the continuum has a limited access and is a step in the right direction. Access to even the rudimentary feelings allows for some connection and working alliance to develop and the coach will be able to sense a baseline of feelings in their coachee. A challenge for this coach is working effectively with leaders who have a broader repertoire of feelings. This coach will likely miss opportunities to notice or sense those feelings and this will diminish the coach's efficacy.

Growing Range of Feelings

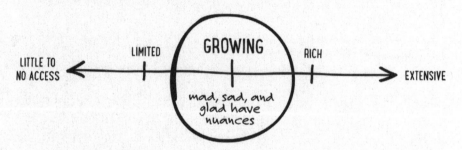

The repertoire is broader. Mad, sad, and glad now have nuances and the coach's feeling vocabulary is enlarged. A coach at this point on the continuum is in an advantageous place, able to build a stronger working alliance, capable of sensing and responding to a wider range of the leader's feelings. The coach with this growing repertoire of feelings is also able to continue to add to their repertoire with more ease as the language of feelings is more accessible for them.

Rich Range of Feelings

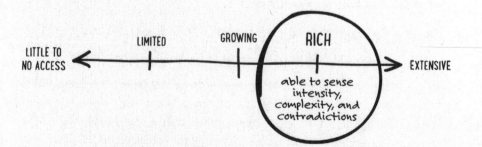

The repertoire is nuanced and rich. The coach is able to sense intensity, complexity and contradictions. The coach with a rich range of feelings is able to build a working alliance with ease and attend to a wide range of feelings with varying levels of intensity, overlap, and nuances.

Extensive Range of Feelings

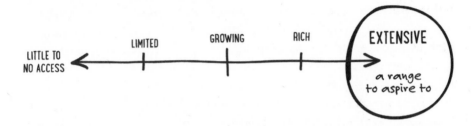

This may be a range to aspire to for all of us and reaching this likely requires one to live a rich life that deliberately engages new experiences and unknown territories and lands. We deepen our range of feelings when we step out of knowing, when we deliberately take some broad leaps into the woods.

Consider these questions to help locate yourself on the feelings spectrum:

- When a coachee sends signals of tearing up in a coaching session, do you stop and explore or keep on topic?
- When a coachee expresses a feeling that is outside of your comfort zone, do you stay there or work to move the conversation in a different direction?
- When a coachee expresses no feelings, do you carry on or stop and see what might emerge?

CULTURE MATTERS

While each of us can likely locate ourselves on this continuum and find edges of development that will enhance our capacity as a coach, there is also an important cultural dimension to our repertoire of feelings that we understand as we coach leaders from diverse backgrounds located around the globe. Emotions and feeling are not reactions to the world we live in; rather, our feelings serve as our construction of the world. Lisa Feldman Barrett's research (2018) on emotions highlights the depth of cultural nuances. Imagine this: the Greeks have a word *stenahoria*, which means a feeling of doom, hopelessness, suffocation, and constriction. Russians have two ways of talking about what Americans call *anger*, Germans have three distinct angers, and Mandarin has five. Greeks have two concepts for guilt that distinguish between minor guilts and major guilts (*enohi*), while Americans have only one. The Dutch culture has an emotion termed *gezellig*, which translates into comfort, coziness, and togetherness at home with friends and loved ones. Danes have what is now a well-known concept, *hygge*, for creating a warm atmosphere and enjoying good things in life with good people. The Inuits have no concept of anger and others have no concept of sadness (Barrett, 2018). As coaches, it is helpful to remind ourselves that emotions and feelings are not universal; they are actually constructed and cultivated in one's culture. Culture wires our brain and is passed on from generation to generation.

DEEPENING YOUR IMPACT: EXPLORING YOUR REPERTOIRE OF FEELINGS

Provoke your brain. Try new experiences and awaken your brain to explore the edges of new feelings and emotions. New experiences can be very simple. The key is trying new experiences regularly to spark your brain. Here are some everyday examples that take little time and few resources:

- Take a walk on a new path you haven't been on before and notice what you see, what feelings are aroused, what surprises you.

- Stay in a conversation with a stranger a few sentences longer.

- Try out a new food or restaurant, especially those you have nearly no experience with.

- Invite a friend for coffee—a friend with whom you don't spend much time.

- Read outside of your comfort zone. If you don't read sci-fi, try it; if you stay glued to nonfiction, try some fiction.

- Try your hand at writing poetry, composing one poem a week for several weeks.

- Watch movies, choosing genres outside of your usual choices.

- Travel to distant lands where you have few, if any, anchors—new language, new landmarks, new customs.

MY INTERNAL LANDSCAPE: STORIES AND STANCES THAT SHAPED MY RANGE OF FEELINGS

When I step back and review milestones and turning points in my own life, I notice how often the feelings associated with these times are complicated. There is never just one feeling; there are often opposing feelings juxtaposed in ways that increase the richness, the intensity, and the poignancy of the moment. I am the mother of three grown sons and there are so many pivots in their lives that aroused a complex range of feelings. In the earliest years, it was the simple act of saying goodbye in the morning as I left for work and they were held by a caregiver, sobbing as though life would end without me. This experience aroused layers of feelings! Or the moment each left home, a wonderful new step ahead that elicited a lot of pride in their accomplishments. It was a profound territory of emotions in which they were ready to spread their wings and I felt a sadness about the ending of a chapter in our lives. As a leader of an organization, a wife, a mother, and an advocate for a just world, I am blessed with the opportunity to be in many settings focused on a broad spectrum of issues and challenges. I work with leaders who are about to engage in a planned departure from a 30-year career and the contours of the experience are complicated. There is joy about retirement, sadness about letting go of a satisfying career, and fear of the unknown. I work with leaders who find themselves midway through their career with what they believed was a clear path forward, when suddenly, unexpected events result in a restructuring and a loss of their role. In these situations, sadness, anger, disbelief, and more emerges. No matter what the specifics of a major and often unexpected change are, the feelings and reactions are most often complicated and require our ability to explore and contain these feelings in our engagements.

FEELINGS ARE FEELINGS

Feelings are feelings. There is no positive/negative sort for feelings. Yet, so often the feelings of joy and happiness are viewed as positive ones we ought all to aspire to; these are the feelings for which we are rewarded and praised. Exhibiting feelings of anger, sadness, and grief are often viewed as *dark* and something we might rather avoid. Every family and every culture has unwritten rules about feelings and as children we learn to adapt in order to flourish or survive in our families and settings. My family was no exception.

Our experiences growing up and the cultural influences of our region in the world influence our range of acceptable emotions, along with the volume and expression of feelings and the levels of intensity allowed when we are children. I grew up on the border of the United States and Canada in the upper Midwest of the country on a cattle ranch and wheat farm. The area was home to mostly second-generation immigrants from Northern Europe, many of whom homesteaded in the area. Winters were long and harsh, large herds of livestock demanded tending no matter what the conditions, seasonal crops required long hours in the fields, neighbors were 100% dependable, and the secret code to surviving and thriving was something like *work hard, help others, and don't complain*, for complaint is viewed as a weaknesses and self-sufficiency is an honored strength. I seldom recall my father getting angry and the only time I saw him shed a tear was when a very close friend of his died unexpectedly. Contrast this with a good friend and colleague of mine who grew up as the youngest in a large Italian immigrant family in an urban area of the East Coast. Her parents ran a lively and boisterous Italian family restaurant where people loved and laughed freely, screamed and shouted together, flew off the handle in anger without warning, and let it go just as quickly.

All feelings were welcome, modeled, and expected, and all ranges of intensity in expression were a part of her growing up experience. Our access to a range of feelings is impacted by our experience growing up, our work experiences, the cultures of the parts of the globe in which we were raised, as well as the deeply embedded DNA of our heritage.

Our histories seem to give valence to feelings, as well; some are viewed as negative while others are deemed positive. Anger, depression, grief, and sometimes sadness are viewed as negative, and when those around us express these feelings many of us want to encourage the other to *look on the bright side*, which is code for *stop talking about these negative emotions*. Happiness, joy, and awe are viewed as positive emotions that are welcomed and good to express in the company of others. Yet, much like the music of a piano, the full range of the keyboard is needed to create music that is complex, rich, and inspiring. We human beings need a full range of emotions to be fully alive. Our times of sadness and grief are woven into the periods of joy and awe in our lives. Each emotion is inextricably connected to another. Anger is the polar opposite of sadness and can help us defend ourselves or serve to motivate us to take active steps to reach an important goal or address a difficult situation. Happiness, or a sense of flourishing, leads to numerous benefits including health, well-being, connectedness, and contentedness.

FEELINGS ARE HUMAN, AND SO ARE LEADERS

Feelings, with their wide range of layers and nuances, are a part of the human condition. When a leader comes to a coach, that person brings all of their self to the work and with this comes feelings. This is not the sole territory of psychotherapy; it is the territory of being human. Often coaches shy away from feelings, worrying this may lead to dark, unknown regions of the psyche. Yet, the way in which we reveal and moderate our feelings is core to who we are as human beings. Our feelings prompt many of our actions and our ability to manage our emotional terrain powerfully impacts who we are, how we are experienced by others, and how we operate in the world. Insights that have the potential to change us and create a breakthrough rarely emerge from the intellect alone. Insights that combine thought and emotions stir and inspire us at a much deeper level. Great coaching requires a coach to have facile access to a wide range of feelings and emotional

Simplishic

experiences. Without this, we will not be able to meet our clients where breakthroughs occur.

At Hudson, I have spent well over three decades working with leaders who enter into our year-long coaching program in order to develop their capacity to coach others. I have worked with leaders from every sector of our business world and observed a broad spectrum of experiences and access to a range of feelings that these leaders bring to the work of coaching. Some bring a limited repertoire while others have deep capacity in this dimension.

I recall a highly skilled tech leader once telling me that he had three go-to feelings—mad, sad, and glad—and that his capacity to traverse these feelings had served him well throughout his career. In contrast, leaders from other sectors, including organization development (OD) and the likes, often enter coaching with heaps of interpersonal work, T-group training, and experiential facilitation; thus, these individuals often have access to a much broader range of feelings. So, our histories, the cultures of our workplaces, and the nature of our work impacts how easily we access our feelings.

THE RANGE OF FEELINGS INVENTORY

It stands to reason that many leaders coming to coaching need to devote energy and focus in building a broader repertoire of feelings to do their best work as coaches. I often suggest a good starting place is to take an inventory of the three areas in Table 6.1.

Once you've explored go-to feelings by using this inventory for a few days and noticed the feelings that are your dominant ones, and you've also tracked those feelings you almost never experience in your day-to-day routines, you are in a position to consciously cultivate a broader range of feelings. While it's true that feelings are neutral, we tend to have judgments about specific feelings. Our judgments can often be tracked to our experiences growing up. The simple act of uncovering judgments allows us to access some of the off-limits feelings and grow our repertoire.

For many of us entering the field of coaching, an important part of our work is broadening our access to feelings and our comfort with an expansive range nuanced with intensity and expression.

Table 6.1   Range of Feelings Inventory

Take an Inventory	What Did You Learn?
First, make a list of all of your go-to feelings, those you gravitate to with ease and regularity. Track yourself for 7–10 days by jotting a list a couple of times each day.	• List the most common feelings you tracked throughout the 7–10 days. • What did you learn about your repertoire?
Next, spend another 7–10 days taking note of your no-go feelings, those you almost never experience in your day-to-day routines.	• List your no-go feelings that are most glaringly missing throughout the 7–10 days. • What did you learn about your repertoire?
Third, spend some time exploring judgments you have about both your go-to feelings and those on the no-go list.	• Are some feelings labeled acceptable or good while others are unacceptable or bad? • What did you learn about yourself and your feelings range?

NO ONE "MAKES US FEEL" ANYTHING!

Years ago, I had the privilege of spending a good deal of time with some of the early founders of Transactional Analysis in the United States, Bob and Mary Goulding. My first experience was in the late 1970s, when month-long T-group experiences were standard in many areas of psychology and psychotherapy training. I remember my first visit at Mount Madonna, a ranch-like setting at the top of a mountain overlooking Monterey Bay on the way up the West Coast of California to San Francisco. Eighteen of us, all psychologists or psychotherapists, arrived to experience group learning in Transactional Analysis (TA) group psychotherapy and the power of full immersion over 30 days and 30 nights. With the exception of Sundays, we spent three group sessions each day together exploring our internal landscape. There are many memorable parts to this long-ago experience and one is about feelings. Often in the group people would say, "she makes me feel ..." and Bob would bellow out across the room,

"Makes you feel? No one makes you feel." He would go on to elaborate on how our reality is that things happen to us and we have a feeling or we decide we have a feeling, but others can never "make us feel." I will never forget this learning. It taught me I am in control of my feelings. I am not a pawn of others. I am able to exercise choices about how I want to respond, and how I want to feel about any given situation.

Karla McLaren (2010) offers a tool she terms *conscious complaining* as a quick practice that yields several helpful results, including learning to recognize and name feelings in order to increase your range of feelings as well as simply expressing feelings in order to cleanse the palette and move on. The practice is a simple one requiring two people—one sharing small complaints and the other listening before exchanging roles. I've used this with great success on multiple occasions. Each time people are initially reluctant to engage in complaining, but after just three to four minutes, they are surprised at how many feelings were lingering outside of their awareness and how energized they are to name them and let them go.

MY INNER LANDSCAPE: WHAT I LEARNED FROM CONSCIOUS COMPLAINING

I put this practice to work with great success not long ago when I was in the midst of recovering from an accident that resulted in a fracture to my spine. Recovery from a fractured spine is at first painful and eventually, a glacially slow healing process that requires going very slowly for many weeks. It required foregoing all the routines I am accustomed to: full work days, lots of travel, teaching, and lecturing for a day or two at a time in front of a group of participants. For three months, all of my routines had to come to an abrupt stop in order to accommodate complete recovery.

The whole scenario required a dramatically slowed pace. One evening nearly a month into this, a colleague stopped by and knowing this was challenging, wondered if I would find it useful to spend a few minutes engaging in conscious complaining. The exercise is short and to the point: focusing on small complaints of the day.

I agreed to give it a try and a long list of complaints unfolded: I can only sleep on my back and I've never slept on my back; I can't bend over so if I drop something I have to ask for help; I need to take naps to help the healing and I've always thought naps were for the undisciplined; I can't drive my car; I can't exercise for three months; I wish I didn't have a set of stairs to climb to get to my bedroom; I can't stand in my kitchen and cook for any length of time; my back is always somewhere between sort of achy and really achy. The list was much longer than I realized and I was surprised by how much better I felt when I acknowledged my list of feelings in the form of small complaints!

DEEPENING YOUR IMPACT: EXPAND YOUR REPERTOIRE OF FEELINGS

Unless you are at the far right of the feelings spectrum, you are probably wondering what one does to build a broader and deeper repertoire. Here are a few practices to build on the previous initial exploration:

- Read, especially memoirs and novels examining the interpersonal domains in depth.

- Check in with yourself regularly and ask, "What feelings have I experienced today?"

- Notice when situations arise and you work to resist or deny feelings.

- Notice when others are expressing feelings, are there some that arouse discomfort in you.

- Take some notes, learn from yourself.

- Watch movies that delve into people's lives in depth.

- Try two minutes of conscious complaining with someone who will listen and ask you *what else*.

THE COACH'S WORKSHEET: DEVELOPING MORE RANGE

Visit www.selfascoach.com for an opportunity to step back from each chapter and reflect on what meaning it has for you and what practices you might develop to keep honing your capacity as coach.

Chapter 7

BOUNDARIES AND SYSTEMS

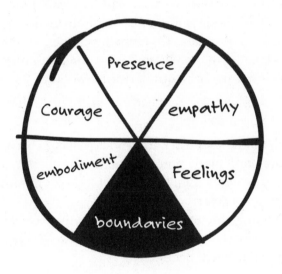

Boundaries don't keep us apart,
they bring us together; they protect us
so we can be safe with another person,
a way of being with each other as equals
so that each stands in the light.

—*Nancy Kline (1999)*

In this dimension of the Self as Coach model, I'm going to artificial-ly pull apart Boundaries and Systems so we can take a look at the nuances before we examine how these are on the same side of the coin.

In the left margin, handwritten: *Disease spread by Clare contract. couples in a unlawful way secret of control.*

THE NECESSITY OF BOUNDARIES

What do you know about your own boundary preferences? How much physical space do you like to have around you—your personal space? How clear are you on what you say *yes* to and what you say *no* to? Is it harder to say yes or no to some people more than others? Do you make decisions by going inside and checking your own rudder or are you often influenced by what others would like?

These questions touch on the outer edges of where our individual boundaries start and stop, how crisp they are, or how much they absorb or hold at a distance the challenges and victories of others. This is where boundaries begin for us as coaches, as well. In this dimension, our ability to hold strong boundaries is intertwined with keeping our empathy balanced. If we absorb (empathy contagion) the experiences of others —taking them on, taking them home, wanting to rescue and alleviate—chances are, our boundaries are wobbly.

Consider the boundaries spectrum in Figure 7.1 and see where you might locate yourself today.

Limited boundaries restrict our work as coaches because when our boundaries are particularly porous we take on others' issues. Alcoholics Anonymous has long used this helpful term for porous boundaries: *collusion*. This term describes the destructive power wherein there are no boundaries, only rescue and agreement in the face of false realities. Collusion is a helpful concept in coaching, as well. When we collude, we ensure no change will occur.

In coaching, when our boundaries are limited and porous, we have an almost automatic tendency to take on what our clients bring to us, to want to solve, to make others feel better, to save them from themselves, to put on the cape and go to work. Ultimately, we lose our coaching rudder and our effectiveness when we are at this end of the spectrum. Through the lens of Horney, this is the red zone wherein we are Moving Toward too much. Our work in coaching is to help our

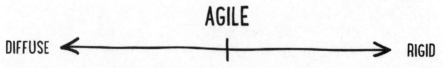

Figure 7.1   Boundaries

clients see their stories and assumptions, not to jump into their situation and become a part of it.

At the other end of the spectrum, when our boundaries are too rigid we run the risk of disconnecting. This links to insufficient empathy; it is Horney's Moving Away stance taken too far and is likely accompanied by a limited range of feelings.

When our boundaries are agile, we are at our best; we are able to hear our client's stories and observe patterns, and to hold a strong alliance while able to surface what we observe instead of getting swept into their situation or story.

MY INNER LANDSCAPE: LEARNING ABOUT SYSTEMS

My first job after completing my master's in psychology was at a community mental health center running therapeutic groups on an inpatient psychiatric ward of a hospital. Like many such facilities in the 1970s, the majority of the population was female, the rate of recidivism was high, and optimal approaches for effective treatment seemed an iffy proposition. Medication regimes combined with time on the unit, some group therapy, and occupational therapy were the tools of the day.

Out of a desire to experiment with new approaches, our team submitted a grant application to the NIMH (National Institute for Mental Health) and received funding to work with the Philadelphia Child Guidance Clinic conducting a two-year study providing systemic family therapy to both the identified patient and all members of the family. Our goal was to create sustainable mental health and reduce the rate of return to the hospital setting. The Philadelphia Child Guidance Clinic was at that time home to the well-known Salvador Minuchin, who along with Jay Haley and others brought family systems therapy into the mainstream in the United States.

THE POWER OF SYSTEMS

The first step was training several of us in a family systems approach. This step was equal parts mind-blowing and transformative for those of us on the team. We initially struggled and resisted as the systems approach turned our thinking upside down relative to the individual-istic patient approach to treatment and the provocative and dynamic work of family systems thinking. As clinicians, we conducted every session behind a one-way mirror with a "bug in the ear" technology, thus allowing another member of our team to intervene with a new approach in the moment in our ear.

To shift gears from an individualistic focus on the patient to a systems approach wherein the identified patient was simply the car-rier of the family pathology was truly a paradigm shift. This systems study taught us all so many lessons: first and perhaps most important-ly, the power of clear boundaries; second, the basic tenets of systems thinking—no blame, no collusion, no triangulation, and ultimately, no revolving door! It taught us how quickly we look for the problem in one person. We identify the issue as a person instead of viewing an issue as systemically based, supported, and sustained because of the dynamics in the system. Read the following vignettes and use them to locate where you would land on the boundary continuum.

Using What's in the Room: When Life Feels Unfair!

Omar arrives at coaching feeling annoyed and shares this scenario with you as the session begins: "I'm in an unfair situation and it's get-ting worse. My co-worker, John, is constantly taking credit for work I initiated, for ideas that came straight from me and what's really mad-dening is that no one else gets this." As his coach, you are listening to your client express his annoyance at the way he has been treated by an-other member of his team: *What happens inside you?* How you man-age your own boundaries makes all the difference. If your boundaries are at the permeable end of the continuum, you could find yourself getting drawn into his story and perhaps wanting to blurt out, "That is outrageous; I can easily see why you are so upset." If you stepped over the boundary and took this approach, you and your client would be engaged in blaming and complaining, but no change would happen. A response wherein you maintain a clearer boundary might be: "So, you feel like you've been treated unfairly and I can tell from the quiver in your voice that even talking about this revives your anger. Could we take this apart a bit and see if there are any adjustments you could make that would change this scenario at all?" In this response with a tighter boundary, you are able to observe Omar's story and mirror it back to him instead of getting drawn into his story.

Using What's in the Room: Work Is Okay but Home Life Is Falling Apart!

Beatta arrives at a coaching session and opens up with the following: "Our focus on my leadership approach is going so well, but honestly what is really getting me down [tears showing up] is my home front. My daughter is sort of . . . well, really out of control. It's her junior year when grades matter, getting into college is a big deal, and instead we are arguing about curfews, parties—we've even had some drinking incidents. The whole situation has me up at night worrying. What do you think I ought to be doing? Have you had any experiences like this with your kids?"

When a client comes to the session hurting and close to tears because of a very tough challenge with one of her children on the home front, what happens next and how you manage your boundaries once again makes all the difference. If you find yourself at the permeable edge of your boundaries and particularly triggered by her tears and sadness, you might find yourself jumping into her story and saying something like, "Wow, I'm so sorry and I've been there with one of my kids. I know how hard it is when something is challenging with our children, but you can't blame yourself and I'm guessing it will turn itself around." Or, a more boundaried response where you can stay out of your client's story might be: "I can hear and see your pain; shall we step back from our work and take a look at what you are up against and see if there are some additional resources that might be useful?"

Again, when our boundaries are wobbly and porous, we get lost in our client's story, drawn into their drama. When our boundaries are firmer, we are able to help the client step back and see their stories and situations with fresh eyes.

Using What's in the Room: The Client Who Frequently Cancels

You are midway into a full day of coaching and in between sessions you pick up this voice-mail message: "Oh, coach, I'm so sorry to do this again but I've got a deadline I didn't see coming and I won't be able to make it today. See you in two weeks." This is the fourth time and each time it is the same day and it throws your schedule off, and frankly, it's annoying. How you approach this issue at your next appointment depends in part upon how you manage your boundaries! If your boundaries are permeable, when your client arrives apologizing for the last cancellation, you'll likely say, "Oh, no worries, I understand things come up," while all the while fuming underneath the surface. If your boundaries are strong, when he arrives and apologizes for the last cancellation, you might say, "I appreciate the apology, but more importantly, I find myself wondering if this happens just with me or if it is something we ought to take a look at that is happening in other places and may be important to our work?"

Permeable boundaries mean we can quickly jump to the other's experience and overidentify with our client, making it difficult to add maximum value in the work. It may mean we are prone to want to make things okay, collude with our client to ensure comfort, or rescue our client, or add value by doing.

Stronger boundaries allow us to consciously notice when we feel tugged to collude, but we resist; when we have an urge to rescue our client, but we resist; or when we want to add value by taking on the work that belongs to our client, but we resist.

ORIGINS OF BOUNDARY MANAGEMENT

Family systems therapist and well-known author on the topic, Murray Bowen (1985), uses the terminology of the differentiated to undifferentiated continuum to explore one's ability to maintain boundaries. He describes the undifferentiated self as the degree of our unresolved emotional attachments to family of origin. He has written, "The degree of unresolved emotional attachment is equivalent to the degree of un-differentiation."

We all operate on a continuum of boundary management: what Bowen referred to as levels of differentiation. Each of us is impacted by our generational history, our family relationships with parents and siblings, and by our own conscious work on self through the course of our adult years.

At our best differentiated self, we have a sense of integration about our self and a belief that we are responsible for our own sense of well-being, our challenges, and our messes. At our lowest level of differentiation, there is much more pervasive experience of anxiety and a sense that others are responsible for our well-being and sense of happiness and contentedness in the world. Check in on your own differentiation orientation. You might pause and consider a recent coaching engagement or two, perhaps one you felt went particularly well and another that was challenging and left you with more questions than answers. As you look through the chart below, you may find that your boundaries are different and your challenges are shifting with different clients. In Table 7.1, which of the experiences are common for you?

We are all somewhere on the path reaching toward increasingly differentiated boundaries. This is a journey for each of us and it is an ethical path, as well. One dynamic we can all count on is the predictability that when under stress, we will be drawn toward a less differentiated place in our self. The trick is in noticing when this occurs.

REDUCING THE URGE TO RESCUE

When our boundaries are balanced—not too rigid nor too porous—our coaching is stronger because we are able to stay out of our client's stories and stances and instead help them see the edges of their stories and patterns. With this balance there is less likelihood we will fall into the rescue trap. The urge to rescue is a trap because we become a part of the client's story instead of helping them see their story. When we rescue, we collude with the client's story and beliefs instead of exploring those beliefs. When we rescue, change does not happen.

Our drive to rescue can be complicated and a common refrain to justify this urge is *I want to add value*. Kets de Vries (2014) adds another perspective, reminding us that often the urge to rescue is fueled by "a disease to please," rendering us ineffective as coaches. Our work is in our ability to step back, pay attention, recalibrate, and move

Table 7.1 Locating Your Boundaries

Diffuse Boundaries (rescue)	Agile Boundaries (responsive)	Rigid Boundaries (rebuff)
• I am immediately drawn into the coachee's story with almost no awareness this is occurring.	• In the midst of a compelling story, I am able to manage my own boundaries and observe the coachee in their story.	• I hear coachee's story, but I don't tap into how it might be to walk in the coachee's shoes, or how this experience might be for her.
• I want to help by taking on what belongs to the coachee.	• I want to be of service by helping the coachee notice patterns, stories, and old habits that need to get realigned.	• I am a bit disconnected from the coachee's story and this limits any tendency to want to help or to carefully notice patterns and stories that are emerging.
• Coachee hurts; I hurt.	• Coachee hurts; I notice and ask about it.	
• Coachee make demands; I want to please.	• Coachee makes demands; I notice whether this is a pattern.	
• Coachee complains; I commiserate.	• Coachee complains; I notice whether this is a pattern.	• Coachee hurts; I might miss this.
• Coachee is chronically late for appointments; I adapt (and feel frustrated or angry) without speaking of it.	• Coachee is chronically late for appointments and after noticing this two or three times, I can trust there is a likely pattern and I bring it up for us to explore together and learn from.	• Coachee makes demands; I don't particularly notice and carry on.
• Reflexively reacting to my inner feeling state without conscious awareness. As I am drawn into the client's story, I notice my urge to help, to make it better, to solve, resolve, reset, and quickly come to the aid of my client.	• Continually noticing what my own internal experience is and instead of reacting, I pay attention to both my feeling state and my intellect.	• Coacheee complains; I don't particularly notice and carry on.
		• Coachee is chronically late for appointments and I mention this and ask coachee to be on time.
		• I am not able to access my internal experience as much as I would like.

forward. Reflection is the first step to change as a coach and as a client. Consider how you would answer these questions today and return to them in a week or two and see if your responses change:

- Do you feel best about yourself when you are helping and attending to others?
- Do you find it difficult to make time for yourself?
- Do you take your client's issues and challenges home with you at end of day?
- Do you have a hard time saying no to a request even when you are not keen on it or it is a serious inconvenience?
- Do you sometimes feel angry or resentful about the time it takes to help another person?
- Do you find yourself at your best when there is a crisis to solve?

SYSTEMS THINKING

> We tend to blame outside circumstances for our problems. "Someone else"—the competitors, the press, the changing mood of the marketplace, the government—did it to us. Systems thinking show us that there is no outside/that you and the cause of your problems are part of a single system. The cure lies in your relationship with your "enemy."
>
> —*Peter Senge (2006)*

When our boundaries are strong it is easier to engage in systems thinking and imagine all parts of the system. Perhaps the most important message in management guru Senge's quote is quite simply that there is no one to blame! In his well-known book about learning organizations, *The Fifth Discipline* (2006), he puts a spotlight on the five essential disciplines including personal mastery, mental models, shared vision, team learning, and systems thinking. Combining Senge's description of systems thinking with the family systems work of Murray Bowen (1985), we can distill the main concepts relevant in coaching, remembering that our exploration of boundaries is interconnected with systems.

SYSTEM'S THINKING CONCEPTS FOR COACHING

The following are general guidelines for how systems thinking and boundary management show up for us in coaching.

- *Homeostasis rules:* This concept originates in the field of biology and it is equally relevant for us as human beings. We seem to gravitate to a static state of being we are accustomed to even in the face of evidence our habits do not serve us best. The gravitational pull toward what we know, our comfort zone, is always at play. This is true for us as coaches and true for our clients. This means that our own resistance to change as well as our client's ought to be expected and appreciated by us as coaches.
- *There is no single root cause, no one to blame:* We human beings imagine that when something goes wrong in our world it is because of someone or something outside of us. Somehow the act of blame is a form of self-vindication that takes us off the hook for exploring our role. Systems thinking challenges us to see the whole system instead of moving to a blame position.
- *Everything is interconnected with everything else:* There are no discrete actions or outcomes inside a system; everything is interconnected. Failures, successes, and learnings are all interconnected and the search for the source is antithetical to systems thinking.
- *Triangles are the basic building blocks:* Once three humans are in place we have a system. Triangles diffuse tension without going to the source, so triangles at play in a system can cause toxicity when allowed to replace straight talk and feedback.
- *Systems have patterns we can learn from:* It is in patterns that the possibility for change arises. Our attention to our own patterns combined with a deep presence allows us to observe patterns in others.
- *Failure is discovery in disguise:* Our best learning comes from our highest quality failures.
- *Small interventions can have a big impact:* All interventions that are workable are small. Change happens in small incremental steps, not in giant leaps.

- *Most of what occurs in systems is not personal:* Some say that at least 80% of what happens in a work environment is not personal and yet we often jump to the conclusion that it is personal and misinterpret what has occurred through our singularly focused lens of self.

Take a look at these short vignettes illustrating some of these systems concepts and see if they sound familiar to you!

"No One Ever Tells Me" or "Systems Have Patterns"

As a leader, one of your valued employees comes to you and complains that he was being left out of the loop, almost suggesting it was a purposeful act delivered in a mean-spirited manner. As you explore the details, a pattern emerges. The team member doesn't ask or request the information he needs but instead waits and hopes someone will bring it to him. Those who have the information find it annoying he doesn't take initiative to get the information. This is an ineffective team pattern and a small systemic intervention made on a few occasions could have a big impact.

"When Sarah Moves Fast, Barrett Moves Slow"; or "Barrett Moves Slow to Manage Sarah's Speed!"

Sarah and Barrett are on an innovations team focused on two important pilot projects. They both find the other's working style a little frustrating and each believes the other is the problem. According to Sarah, she thinks quickly and likes to iterate rapidly and when she brings her ideas to Barrett he puts the brakes on and all of a sudden, she has to figure out how to manage Barrett instead of moving the project forward. Barrett sees it quite the opposite. He believes Sarah moves way too quickly and makes mistakes that ultimately slow them down if they go unchecked; so, he has adopted an approach of slowing down in order to manage her speed, hoping to increase the likelihood of success of their project. Systems have patterns we can learn from.

"Yes, I Really Do Want to Change"

Uri comes to coaching knowing he needs to make some changes if he is going to get the promotion he dearly wants. He has been passed over three times and he's started to realize he plays a role in this, and he must have a blind spot. He comes to coaching to focus on increasing his approachability and connection. You do a series of stakeholder interviews and his original goal is confirmed as the important one, and the lack of approachability and connection is even greater as viewed by his stakeholders than he perceives. The work proceeds and even while Uri says he wants to change, even while you've jointly crafted some action steps that will increase his way of being with others, each week he returns to coaching and nothing has changed. Homeostasis rules! Until Uri and the coach can uncover the obstacles getting in the way of adjusting his behavior, the homeostasis will prevail.

DEEPENING YOUR IMPACT: BUILDING MORE DIFFERENTIATION

Practice	Impact
Notice where the boundaries are in your day-to-day life.	This is the first practice in building even stronger boundaries and deepening your differentiation. We are often so wrapped up in the business of our daily routines that we are not aware of how many boundary opportunities there are for us to stand at the edge of with more clarity and certainty.
Stay out of other people's stories so you can be fully present for them as you listen.	Notice the triggers that start to draw you in and use the triggers to signal stepping back, pausing, taking a breath, and re-centering.

Keep communication clean by de-triangulating.	Make an agreement with yourself to practice speaking directly to the person you are troubling about and avoid talking with a third party about the other person. The impact is immediate. Nothing changes when we talk to one person about another – it's just a way of letting off steam, complaining, or blaming.
Get clear on your yeses and nos.	Peter Block has long said, "Your yeses don't mean anything until you can say no." Saying no when it matters is a good way of practicing clear boundaries. All too often, many of us say yes when we would like to say no, and the impact on us and others can be significant in bad feelings, resentments, and unspoken bargains.
Know what matters to you at this time in life.	When we are fuzzy about the future, where we are going, and what matters most, our boundaries get blurry and we can find ourselves led by someone else's agenda.

THE COACH'S WORKSHEET: DEVELOPING MORE RANGE

Visit www.selfascoach.com for an opportunity to step back from each chapter and reflect on what meaning it has for you and what practices you might develop to keep honing your capacity as coach.

APPLYING HEAT: CASE VIGNETTE II

CASE VIGNETTE #2: OVERWORKED AND OUT OF CONTROL

You've entered into a coaching engagement with Jana, a leader in her early thirties who has recently been promoted to a senior director role. She arrives at coaching excited about her new role and wanting to take a look at what she will need to adjust to hit this new role "out of the park." She has spent her career in the tech industry and is smart and accomplished in this domain.

What unfolds in the discovery portion of the coaching is a picture of Jana working all hours, all days, all the time. She describes her life as "riding a train that is always on the verge of being out of control." While her academic and work history are stellar, she describes an underlying insecurity about being able to hit the mark, driving her to overwork, taking on too much, and resorting to overly controlling behaviors in an attempt to hit that mark.

Over the course of the first several sessions, what you've noticed is a sensation that you, too, are on a train that is on the verge of going out of control! Each session, as you attempt to zero in and focus on what the client articulates as the most important work, it seems there is another fire that has shown up and Jana wants to refocus on it. Unlike most coaching, at the conclusion of these sessions you notice a sensation of feeling drained.

Here's how three different coaches might approach this situation with the lens of each of the Self as Coach domains applied to enhance the applicability and relevance of the model.

Coach 1

Coach 1 wonders if he missed something in the early contracting conversation about what coaching is and how it unfolds. He worries that what Jana wants from him as coach is to simply help her put out fires and move from one issue to another in each session. He believes he has built trust and respect and he feels Jana's pain relative to her nearly out-of-control train and her underlying insecurity. He is concerned he is not helping her, and he finds himself worried about her between sessions.

Where Coach 1 Is in Each of the Six Dimensions

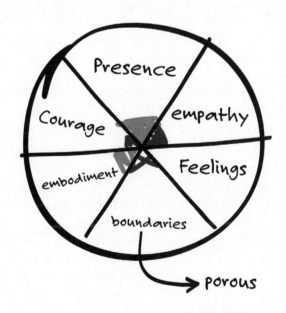

Presence. The coach finds himself distracted by his inner chatter and this has the natural potential to reduce his presence. This limited presence makes it difficult for a coach to pay full attention to what is unfolding in the session.

Empathy. The coach reflects on his working alliance and believes he has developed a strong connection. This all-important connection will prove invaluable as the coaching unfolds.

Range of Feelings. The coach seems able to contain the client's feelings and this, again, allows the client to explore what is most important to her in the coaching engagement.

Boundaries and Systems. The coach finds himself a bit drawn into his client's situation and notes that he wants to help her and worries about her between sessions. Once drawn into the client's story and sense of urgency, the coach is likely rendered less effective in helping the client observe herself and her story.

Embodiment. The coach doesn't offer any comments relative to his physical stability or how centered and grounded he feels during the sessions.

Courage. The coach is able to notice the overarching themes and patterns of fires and the train she references, but his desire to help her (getting drawn into her story) makes it difficult for him to step out on the balcony and share observations and patterns that might prove useful to his client.

Coach 2

Coach 2 finds that it takes conscious work to stay present and centered in the presence of this client and when he accomplishes this, he sees a powerful connection between the metaphor she describes — riding a train that is on the verge of being out-of-control — and the experience he has as Jana arrives at coaching with another fire she is putting out and wanting to talk about with him. While he believes he has a good working alliance with Jana, he worries about how he might surface this connection with Jana without making her feel badly, especially in light of what she has shared about feeling inadequate.

Where Coach 2 Is in Each of the Six Dimensions

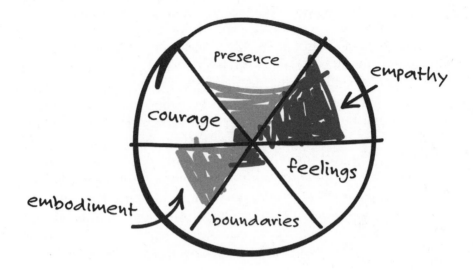

Presence. The coach tells us he is actively engaged in being present and he mentions his presence increases his ability to see more clearly connections between what the client describes and how she shows up in the coaching sessions. When our presence is strong, we observe the moment and our client with increased clarity; we notice nuances of language, patterns, somatic signals, and more.

Empathy. The coach believes the working alliance is strong and this enables him to explore with the client what is most important.

Range of Feelings. The coach doesn't reference the feelings domain, but given his presence and empathy are strong, one might expect his range of feelings has been cultivated, as well.

Boundaries and Systems. The coach finds himself a bit drawn into his client's situation and notes that he finds he is worrying about making her feel badly. Once drawn into the client's story, he is likely rendered less effective in helping the client observe herself and her story.

Embodiment. The coach mentions his conscious intentions around getting present and centered in these sessions.

Courage. The coach is able to notice the overarching themes and patterns of fires and the train she references, but his worries about making her feel badly (getting drawn into the client's story) limit his use of courage in sharing observations that might prove helpful to this client.

Coach 3

Coach 3 believes he has developed strong rapport with Jana and he finds her ability to viscerally describe her experience—the intensity, the almost-out-of-control train, the underlying insecurities—a real support in being able to explore this terrain together. He finds himself experiencing a parallel train ride, much like she describes, each time their coaching session unfolds. When he believes his connection is strong enough he shares this parallel observation. He is particularly careful to share it with heart because of all she has shared about her insecurities. The first time, he says something like, *You mention this experience of traveling on a nearly out-of-control train, such a helpful description and observation and, you know, I find myself sharing that experience as you bring in these important situations that are on your mind. I wonder if you notice this intensity in our discussion as we talk? I wonder if there are any ways we might look at this together?*

Where Coach 3 Is in Each of the Six Dimensions

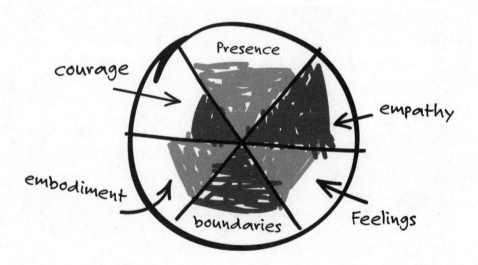

Presence. The coach appears to be fully present and able to reflect in the moment about what is unfolding.
Empathy. The coach reflects on his working alliance and self-assesses that he has developed a strong rapport. This proves essential in deeper explorations.

Range of Feelings. The coach seems able to fully appreciate his client's feelings as well as reflect on his own. This allows the client to go where it is most important in the coaching engagement.

Boundaries and Systems. The coach finds himself a bit drawn into his client's situation and notes that he has an urge to help her, but he resists by strengthening his boundaries and this allows him to *get on the balcony* (more on this in Chapter 7) and observe patterns and stories that may prove helpful to the client.

Embodiment. The coach doesn't offer any reflections relative to how centered and grounded he might be during the sessions, yet his approach suggests he is able to find ways to keep himself grounded.

Courage. The coach is able to notice the overarching themes and patterns of fires and the train she references, and he is able to step out on the balcony and share observations that might prove useful to his client.

Chapter 8

EMBODIMENT

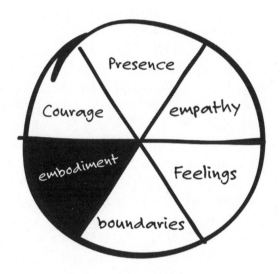

The body is incapable of not practicing. And what we
practice we become.
Even as you sit here reading ... you are shaping yourself by
your posture, the way you're breathing, what you're thinking,
feeling and sensing.
While this may seem subtle and far below the level of our
awareness, over time this has a powerful effect on how we
perceive the world and how the world perceives us.
—*Richard Strozzi-Heckler (2014)*

Every action we take originates in our body. Our thoughts, our
words, our actions—we cannot produce an action without
involving our body. It follows, then, that in order to change we need to

engage our body. As Wendy Palmer (2013) so aptly writes, "The way we sit and stand can change the way we think and speak." The goal of being an embodied coach inspires us to cultivate our ability to be present to our whole self: head, heart, and gut. A coach able to ground oneself and remain centered in the midst of difficult times and challenging engagements is equipped to manage whatever presents itself in the coaching engagement.

I freely admit I have been slower than most to experience the wisdom of my body. I was one of those who revered the mind and thought my body was just along for the journey. Today, I find enormous value in cultivating my embodied self, engaging in daily centering practices, and learning from the wisdom of my body that often far exceeds my mind! My revelations about my mind-body disconnect happened a few years in a most unusual way well outside the bounds of coaching. I have been exploring the world of clay, pottery wheels, and kilns for nearly a decade. My progress is slow, in part because I am only able to devote small chunks of time to this work because of other commitments in my life, but what seems to impede me even more than time is myself, my way of connecting to the clay, and the work. Like any learning, the power of a great teacher or mentor is immeasurable, and over the past two or three years, I had the gift of two such teachers. One, in particular, had the knack of combining candor with light humor and the combination is just enough to create small cracks in my old habits that allow for new learning and far better ceramics!

GET OUT OF YOUR HEAD!

I have heard this message—"Get out of your head, Pam"—bellow from my ceramics teacher from across the room over and over in the past couple of years. Other students in the studio snicker a bit and initially, I cringed wondering what, precisely she wanted me to do. Now, I get it. My goal in my work at this stage is simple and seemingly impossible. I want to throw the clay in such a way that I am able to pull up broad, thin walls. What I've learned is that in order to execute this simple yet difficult act I need to be fully grounded in my body, the tips of my fingers, my breathing, and my posture. When I am in my head judging my work, planning for how it will look or dreaming about a stunning bowl, things go badly! When I am in my body, magic happens; I feel the rhythm of the water racing through my fingers as I slowly draw the sides of a bowl up and out. I am centered in my body, spellbound by the power of this sort of presence to the moment, to the clay, the water, and the hum of the wheel.

In my first years of sitting at the wheel and attempting to throw a pot, my body was completely disconnected from my brain, my thoughts were in charge, and my body was in a habit. When I am in this new centered and embodied state in the studio, everything changes inside me and in the work I am able to do. This is true whether creating a bowl in the studio, coaching a client, or living our day-to-day lives. M.C. Richards long ago wrote a wonderful book I regularly reread: *Centering: In Pottery, Poetry and the Person* (1964). It's about pottery, our bodies, and our humanness, and it parallels our work as coaches beautifully. Here is my favorite quote from the book:

> As human beings functioning as potters, we center ourselves and our clay. We know how necessary it is to be "on center" ourselves if we wish to bring our clay into center. Tensions in the fingers, in the arms and back, holding the breath, these things count. The potter has to prepare her body as she does that of the clay.

Powerful words from M.C. Richards; they suggest that to do our work, we need to be centered and we need to embody our self, whether as a potter, a coach, or a leader. The realm of embodiment and somatic awareness is also inextricably connected to presence: presence to our inner chatter and presence to the third entity. The potter's chatter is often in the form of: "My wall is too thin, my clay feels off center, I'm working too slowly, and I'm pulling too quickly." It's the same in whatever our art is—our internal chatter throws us off center.

When coaching, how often have you lost your center by asking one or more of the following of yourself?

- Am I asking the right question?
- Am I hitting the mark for my client?
- Wow, my client's perceptions seem way off. How and what would be my best move here?
- I'm aware of feeling annoyed. How do I get my self back to us?

This is where my ceramics teacher, if a master coach, might holler, "Get out of your head!" This is the power of developing practices that allow us to observe ourselves. Our brain is connected to our body. Sensations are experienced first in our body and only later interpreted in our brain. Yet, many of us worship the brain and ignore the wisdom of our body. Embodiment is all about how we live in our body and allow our body to be the center from which we interact and move in the world.

HONING OUR *FELT SENSE* AND OUR SOMATIC MARKERS

Allowing our body to be the center from which we interact requires us to hone a felt sense of our self. Scientists often refer to this as *proprioception*: the ability to sense and respond to stimuli in our body without the aid of our visual perceptions. This is sometimes described as a *sixth sense*.

SOMATIC MARKERS

Antonio Damasio (1994) coined the term *somatic markers* to suggest feelings in our body are connected with particular emotions. If we are living mostly in our head and disconnected from our body, the chances are our associated emotions are a combination of stress, rushing, planning, worrying, and so on. The ingrained ways our unique bodies each respond to life, stress, and the unexpected is built into our muscle memory and the way we hold ourselves. Some of us may shrink, cave in our shoulders a bit; others may puff up the chest; some of us enter a difficult conversation with a frown or an over-smile. Whatever our conditioned responses or somatic markers might be, they are cultivated over time, connecting sensations to feelings and causing a certain set of muscles to contract or a particular posture to be assumed, or a way of breathing (shallow, slow, quick) to take hold. We tell a story about ourselves through these markers and as Wendy Palmer reminds us, "The way we sit and stand can change the way we think and feel." In other words, our emotions ultimately create the shapes we become as adults.

What a loss it would be for us in our own development as coaches and in our work with our clients if we ignored the wisdom of our body and insufficiently cultivated attunement to our felt self; and what a loss for our clients if we are unable to harvest the wisdom of the body to support our work.

The work of those who have dedicated themselves to this field of study seems to reliably draw our attention, first, to the shape of our self—our somatic markers. Finding our breath, using our breath to center and ground ourselves, and integrating all of this allows us to reliably return to our body as our main source of wisdom and feedback.

BECOMING SELF-GENERATIVE

Doug Silsbee (2008) explained it this way: "When we are self-generative, we have the capacity to be present and a learner in all of life in order to make choice from the inner state of greatest possible awareness and resourcefulness." The ability to be self-generative significantly increases our capacity as coaches to be resilient, fully aware, and awake and ready to learn again.

Centering Ourselves

Centering is an internal practice of bringing our full attention to our body and all of our body's sensations, aligning our body to the three dimensions of space in which we live: depth, length, and width. There are many variations on this centering practice, and it's probably optimal when we each customize it to make it work best for one's self. With each of these three dimensions, I'm including a practice to experiment with. However, know most of all that this needs to work for you.

First, Finding Our Length and Our Dignity

Most of us are physically aligned to what we've become accustomed to over years of habits, including any variety of stories—the head is well in front of the body, the shoulders are collapsed, the gut is forward of the head, head and shoulders are leaning back. It takes the eye of a keen observer to help us see where we are out of alignment as we work to find our length. The rhythm is extending upward and relaxing downward. Lengthening and softening repeatedly.

A Practice for Finding Our Length

This particular practice is one I came across while reading Peter Hamill's book, *Embodied Leadership: The Somatic Approach to Developing Your Leadership* (2013). This same practice likely occurs in several other sources, as well.

First, finding your length by standing up with feet about shoulder-width apart, arms by your sides and eyes wide open. Imagining a string threaded through your body elongating your spine upward and relaxing downward feeling the power of gravity, too.

Next, Hamill offers the image of a series of bands we have running up and down our body from top of head to bottom of feet. We each loosen and tighten these bands through our experiences, emotions, and habits, so the practice of slowly experiencing each band can reveal some of our best honed habits. A stop at each band allows you to notice any tension, to experiment with releasing tension and to perhaps notice some bodily nuances often outside your awareness.

At each stop you might practice holding tension and releasing a few times to see what you notice:

- *Band One*: The Forehead—Some of us hold a lot of tension in this area either with furrowed brows that can give the message of worry or anger, or raised brows that might signal surprise or fear to others.
- *Band Two*: The Eyes—The level of tension or relaxation in our eyes takes many forms: hard eyes, glazed, peering or searing, and open and relaxed.
- *Band Three*: The Jaw—This powerful muscle is capable of holding so much tension it can result in teeth gnashing in the night. When the jaw is fully relaxed our back teeth are not touching. This leaves the mouth just slightly ajar. When we hold a lot of tension in our jaw, our lips purse a bit—hence the phrase *grin and bear it*.
- *Band Four*: The Shoulders—Another common place to store tension whether it is that our shoulders are raised up nearly touching our ears or our arms are held out from the sides of

our bodies; both of these positions take a good deal of energy to maintain.

- *Band Five*: The Chest—Some of us collapse our chest or jut out the chest and either requires energy, making it difficult to maintain access to our heart.
- *Band Six*: The Stomach—Often a place in our body where we hold emotions. Finding ways to soften, and imagining a *soft belly* allows us to let go of added tension.
- *Band Seven*: The Sphincters—Another common place to hold tension, we often use the term *anal* to suggest someone who is uptight. Imagine loosening these muscles.
- *Band Eight*: The Legs—Tension is often stored in locked knees that make it harder for us to relax our legs. Practicing a softening of the knee loosens tension we might hold here.
- *Band Nine*: The Feet—Tension is often evidenced in continual tapping and moving of the feet. Letting go of this attention allows us to feel the Earth and let gravity support us more fully.

Standing tall and relaxing downward into the body. Imagine taking the few minutes needed to do a body scan of these nine bands a few times each day. Imagine what you would learn about where you store your tensions and how you might change the way you stand if some of that tension were released even just a bit.

Second, Finding Our Width and Our Connectedness

Pay attention to the space on either side of yourself: your width. Experiment with how much space you take up out of habit and whether or not you would like to broaden your width or pull it in a bit. This is our social dimension, our connectedness with others. If we use very little of our width, we may have a tendency to play it too small in our own world, and if we use too much we may veer into the space of others.

A Practice for Finding Our Width

Rock side to side and gain a sense of the comfort zone of your space and your width. Do this several times throughout the day for a few days, noticing where your natural comfort zone seems to be.

Third, Finding Our Depth, Our Support, Our Ancestry

Find the balance point between present and future. Rocking gently back and forth can help to locate your balance point. Too often we are focused on what is in front of us but we ignore the space behind us. Doug Silsbee (2008) had this wonderful metaphor for the space behind us: He termed it "our dinosaur tail," meaning our history, our ancestors, our heritage, our culture, and all who have supported and continue to support us in the world.

A Practice for Finding Your Depth

Who's got your back today and through the ages? Metaphorically, who can you lean on today and in your history; who is in your "dinosaur tail"? Take some time to reflect on this. Make a list of those from your ancestry, those in your past and those today, some who know you well and some who may be iconic figures you admire by virtue of their example in the world.

Centering and grounding ourselves and focusing on our length, width, and depth is a practice we can engage in that allows us to consciously embody our self. This is a place to start and a place to stay in this work.

THE COACH'S WORKSHEET: DEVELOPING MORE RANGE

Visit www.selfascoach.com for an opportunity to step back from each chapter and reflect on what meaning it has for you and what practices you might develop to keep honing your capacity as coach.

Chapter 9

COURAGE

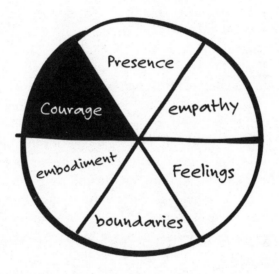

You cannot swim for new horizons
until you have the courage to
lose sight of the shore.

—*William Faulkner*

COURAGE HAS MANY FORMS

Faulkner says it well—it takes courage for us to lose sight of our shores.
If we don't let go of what we know, our capacity to reach new horizons
is greatly constrained. This concept of courage has roots in our earliest
recorded human writing and the meaning of the concept has depth
and nuance. Today, writer and philosophy professor Daniel Putnam

(2004) considers three kinds of courage: physical, moral, and psychological. It is the third kind that we will look at most closely for its relevance to the work of coaching.

First, a few words about physical and moral courage. Physical courage was at the heart of the ancient Greek sagas of courage in the tales of Odysseus and others. Odysseus's courage was predominantly of a physical nature, as it entailed enduring a 10-year struggle to return home to Ithaca following the Trojan War. Each stop along his journey was fraught with physical dangers requiring enormous courage as he battled mythical beasts and the ire of the gods. Modern-day versions of physical courage are equally daunting. Think of the courage of the 70 million refugees in our world today who continue to put another foot forward walking across continents, searching for a safe place to exist.

Moral courage is the kind fueled by a passion and commitment to an ethical compass deep within. Nelson Mandela was among icons demonstrating this sort of extraordinary courage. He became the first black president of South Africa after spending 27 years in prison where he was confined to a small cell without a bed or plumbing, forced to do hard labor in a lime quarry. Upon release, he promoted a message of forgiveness and equality throughout the culturally torn country. The recipient of the 1993 Nobel Peace Prize, he is often quoted as saying, "There is no passion to be found playing small, in settling for a life that is less than the one you are capable of living." Malala Yousafzai was only 15 years old when she demonstrated remarkable courage as a gunman boarded her school bus in Pakistan shouting her name. Instead of endangering others and remaining silent, she stood up and said, "I am Malala," whereupon he shot her three times in the head. Miraculously, she recovered and continues to demonstrate enormous courage based on her moral convictions. Malala is often quoted as saying, "I raise up my voice not so I can shout but so that those without a voice can be heard . . . we cannot succeed when half of us are held back." In 2014, Yousafzai received the Nobel Peace Prize.

PSYCHOLOGICAL COURAGE

The third form of courage is a psychological courage, described as "overcoming the fear of losing the psyche, the fear of psychological death" (Putman, 2004). This form can also be characterized as the willingness and courage to face up to our inner fears and long-held habitual ways of being. This psychological courage is most relevant to our work as coaches because to do our best work, we need a willingness to confront our own fears in order to be of service to our clients.

The work we do and the relationships we forge with our clients demand the best of what we are capable of as coaches. Leaders seek coaching because they want to make some changes pivotal to their way of being as a leader, changes that they are simply unable to live into on their own. Why? Because like us, they are human and unable to fully grasp or gain a view of their blind spots, well-worn patterns, and the habits that served them in the past and hinder them now. To meet leaders where they need us most, to reach for new horizons with our clients, requires us to be courageous. We are traveling together in new territory, uncovering old, mostly invisible habits and stories, and examining together things that have been unspoken. This work is not for the faint of heart!

CULTIVATING OUR COURAGE

Our willingness and capacity to cultivate courage is one of the hallmarks distinguishing good coaches from great ones. To have courage as a coach we need to bring all of the other elements of Self as Coach to bear:

- We need our full presence to spot opportunities to exercise courage in our coaching.
- Well-balanced empathy allows us to express a courageous comment or observation with heart in a way that invites the client to consider it.
- Access to the range of feelings expressed by the client allows us to meet the client where they are.
- Strong boundaries prevent us from getting drawn into the client's story and instead courageously observe the story so the leader and coach can learn together.
- Centering ourselves and focusing on embodiment allows us to stay strong and attuned, and provides a steady support when we feel wobbly about proceeding when the stakes are highest.

Throughout the exploration of Self as Coach, I have often used the phrases "using what's in the room" and "turning up the heat." These phrases signify our ability to use courage as an access point to create the conditions for change to unfold. Both using what's in the room and turning up the heat act as courageous invitations for our client to see something about self with fresh eyes or first eyes.

MY INTERIOR JOURNAL: WHAT I'VE LEARNED ABOUT THE POWER OF COURAGE

I will forever remember working with a coach in the midst of some tough and tricky situations that had emerged early in my role as a leader. I was so certain the issues at hand were not mine, and I was probably exhibiting that righteous indignation that can show up at these times! My coach stopped me and with heart and lightness asked me, "Do you notice what you are saying? *It's all about others.* I wonder what this says about you and if you are willing to take that path for a bit, as well." Powerful, courageous, and inviting. The moment turned out to be pivotal in changes I made in my leadership style and monumental in how I viscerally understood the power of courage. There are so many ways she might have made this observation or shared a pattern she was seeing in my words and she chose heart, lightness, and an invitation. No judgments, no challenging my thinking, no rescuing me, no triangulating. She used what was in the room in that moment and turned up the heat in a manner that allowed me to step into new possibilities.

OUR COURAGE CREATES AN INVITATION

The question of what is demanded of us as coaches in order to engage in courageous acts in our work is deeply personal. That which is personal leads back to our own attachment styles, level of development, and willingness to engage in our vertical development. In other words, have we cultivated our internal landscape sufficiently to allow us to develop our courage? Courage grows in the choices we make and the actions we undertake every day in our work. Our willingness to speak our truth, to share an important perspective or observation, to be candid when it matters, or to be provocative in order to help a client gain another perspective—these are acts of courage, demonstrations of going bigger, and signs of resisting the urge to retreat to the shore and avoid the new horizons. A coaching colleague and master coach, Tom Pollack, has often said, "Courage is an invitation that taps you on the shoulder during a coaching session and says, 'Bring this up with the client,' even though you would prefer staying safe in the moment." The truth is, when we refuse the invitation to step into that courageous space with our clients, both of us lose.

DEEPENING YOUR IMPACT: BUILDING MORE COURAGE

- Pay attention to patterns that emerge in the situations and stories discussed in coaching and find ways to bring up what you notice using heart and courage.

- Build comfort in sharing observations that stand out in a coaching session—things like making little eye contact, watching one's smartphone, constantly tapping a foot, apologizing repeatedly, using a phrase (*I'm just not lucky*, etc.) with a high frequency, showing up late to several coaching calls, continually cancelling coaching sessions, and so on.

- Develop ease using what's in the room and exploring this with the client. This might be pointing out how a client moves rapidly from one topic to another in a disjointed way or talks in a circular manner making it harder to connect the links.

- Practice using silence as a way to create a bit of heat that will often give the client enough needed time to uncover something important that might not surface if we fill these spaces with small talk or comments.

FEAR AND LETHARGY THWART COURAGE

For many years, our team of faculty at Hudson has come together for an annual retreat to renew, recalibrate to be at our best in our coaching work with others, and learn from a master. At a recent retreat, we spent a day with one of those masters, James Hollis, well-known Jungian analyst, professor, and author of numerous books. He focuses on the complicated internal landscape of humans and threads the concept of courage throughout his work. On that day, Hollis modeled courage as he boldly provoked and prodded precious beliefs and biases we held about our lives. One story he shared linking to courage goes something like this (sic): "Every morning when we awaken and look about scanning our surroundings to find our bearings, we are confronted with two beasts at the foot of our bed, comfortably perched on each of the bed posts. One beast is LETHARGY and the other is FEAR." Each day as we awaken we make choices about whether to cave to the powerful forces of one or both of these beasts, whether to slump back a bit and take the easier road that doesn't require so much of us. The voice of *fear* encourages us to stay small and cautions us that we are not prepared to take any risks. The voice of *lethargy* is, in Hollis's words, the more seductive one telling us to chill out, we've done enough, take it easy, have a glass of wine, watch a sitcom, that's good enough. There is a universality about the voices of lethargy and fear we all share. Growing our psychological courage requires that we wake up to our internal voices and the messages of fear and lethargy that sustain old habits and routines.

LEARNING TO ROCK THE BOAT

Our capacity to develop a heightened awareness of these two beasts that seem to magnetically pull us toward comfort, habit, and safety, is one of the important ways we build our psychological courage, that essential cornerstone in great coaching. The coach may have a fear of rocking the boat when the engagement is mostly going just fine; or they may fear that a courageous comment could alter the relationship and the client's view of the coach; or they may have a fear that says, I, *as coach, will not be liked as much by my client, or a bold comment could ruin my rating or risk additional work.* The bedpost of lethargy continually tugs at us and the familiar inner chatter is saying, *Why take the risk? I'm at home with my current approach. Why take a chance? This is good enough as is.*

Building the capacity to call on our courage comes with time, experience, collegial and supervisory input, and life experiences. In Hollis's most recent book, *Living an Examined Life: Wisdom for the Second Half of the Journey* (2018), he offers series of 21 desiderata to courageously make our life more of our own with a stronger sense of agency and a willingness to play bigger and risk more. His opening desiderata is provocative for all of us: *Grow Up*. Whatever it is we are shirking away from, whenever we find our old habits and ways of being sufficient in this world, we are taking the easy path. *Grow Up* can remind us as coaches that we need to ground ourselves in our values and go bigger, lean into the unknown, and resist the call of lethargy.

Often our opportunities to grow up, stay awake, and demonstrate courage are found in small micro-moments of everyday life. When we are alert to these moments and we lean into them we strengthen our courage muscle. It may be that small moment of providing feedback to another that may be hard to hear, or that opportunity to take a stand on an issue that matters to you, or the willingness to offer an opposing view in the face of disagreement. Courage requires that we set boundaries and say no when it matters. It takes courage to say no and sometimes even more to say yes.

DEEPENING YOUR IMPACT: RECALL SMALL ACTS OF COURAGE

You can likely scan the last few months and identify moments of courage, small acts that required you to take a stronger stand than usual. Perhaps it was a refusal, a *no* to a request, or a decision to take action that rested on your shoulders, or a *yes* to leading an initiative that's a little outside your comfort zone. These small acts of courage are supported by our values, ethics, and sense of what matters most at this time in your life. Then there are the larger acts. Taking a public stand in the face of opposition, leaving a great work role to pursue a risky dream, setting a very tough limit with a family member. The continual cultivation of small acts makes the bigger ones possible.

LEADERS NEED COURAGEOUS COACHES

Leaders seek out a coach because something is not working as well as they and others would like it to work. Leaders come to us because stakeholders have put a spotlight on a blind spot that is a barrier to success. They appear out of a desire to continue to grow in their roles and career paths and often the obstacles and blind spots are not at all clear to them. If these leaders could pick up a book, an article, or a tool and rapidly make the adjustments they need to live into, they would be doing so! It takes courage for a leader to seek out a coach and when a leader comes knocking, they deserve the coach's courage to help them look at that which is invisible or only marginally accessible and uncomfortable to explore. This is what others do not and will not do; this is what is needed to help leaders grow and deepen their capacities and this requires grit and courage on your part as a coach.

TURNING UP THE HEAT AND DEMONSTRATING COURAGE IN OUR COACHING

Demonstrating courage takes many forms in our work as coaches. In Table 9.1, I expand on a handful of common courage pivots.

Table 9.1   Common Pivots to Courage in Coaching

Common Coach Scenarios	Coaching + Courage	Impact on Coachee's Development: A Coach's Reflections
	• Sharing an observation	
	• Using what's in the room	
	• Turning up the heat	
	• Being transparent	
	• Noticing a pattern	

Late Again

The client routinely shows up late for appointments and cancels from time to time at the last minute.

"John, I've been noticing something I think could be useful for us to explore—are you up for that? Great. Over the past two months you have been 15–20 minutes late for most of our sessions, twice you've canceled at the very last minute. It's got my attention because it is such a regular occurrence and I wonder if what is happening here might be worth some exploration. Are you up for that?"

John expressed surprise and little awareness of his lateness behavior. While I shared how it impacted me, I put a bigger focus on wondering how it might be occurring with his team and wondering what impact that might have. This opened the door to a pivotal focus on how he shows up as a leader of his team, how his team experiences his routine tardiness, and the powerful message embedded in this behavior that was out of his awareness.

The Talking Is Non-Stop

The client has a habit of talking nonstop almost without taking a breath, adding one sentence after another and in the process making it hard to track what's important or at the core.

"Marge, could I stop you for a moment and ask you to step back for a bit and reflect?" I'm aware that you've been talking pretty much non-stop for the past several minutes and I'm starting to get lost. I find myself wondering if you have an awareness of this and if we might this explore together?"

Marge wants to be considered for a promotion and she has received feedback she does not show up as a leader. Turns out her habit of talking nonstop thoroughly diminished her presence and others lost interest in what she was saying. The courage to use what was in the room and explore the pattern the coach observed was a turning point in the work.

(continued)

Common Coach Scenarios	Coaching + Courage	Impact on Coachee's Development: A Coach's Reflections
It's All About Me, Me, Me The client has a habit of bringing everything we explore back to himself, using himself as the reference point for all that he experiences and describes.	Jack, you've said a lot about you, could we step back and play with what you imagine this is like for the four folks on your senior team?	Jack wants to be a strong and respected leader of his team. His stakeholder feedback has a singular theme: *It's always about Jack.* When we reviewed the feedback, he was surprised and not aware of this dynamic. The courage to share this in the session allowed Jack to get a glimpse of what his people experience.
I'm Hearing Victim-Talk This client is unable to see her role in situations that occur within her team. She finds it easier to blame than take responsibility for what she might be contributing to the situations.	Anu, I wonder if you would allow me to share a pattern I'm hearing often over these last three sessions? I hear you saying things like, "Why do bad things always happen to me?" or "I just have a lot of bad luck." These are powerful statements—I wonder if you are aware of how often you say these to yourself?	Anu's inability to see her victim-like language in the coaching conversation provides powerful input into a blind spot that she hasn't seen. Left unchecked, her development will be stunted.

That Pace Is Intense

This client arrives at coaching concerned that he is not getting advancements he would like and unable to see what the obstacles might be. Stakeholder input centered around his pace and intensity.

Coach: Steve, would you allow me to share what I'm noticing?

Steve: Sure, go ahead.

Coach: I keep noticing this intensity in your voice as you speak— your voice is strong, loud, and there is a pressured quality, a speed at which you speak. I notice my own heart rate picks up and I start to feel a little anxiety internally and I wonder if this happens in other places and if it's worth our exploration?

Steve: Wow, I'm really not aware of what you describe, but it is similar to what showed up when you did my stakeholder interviews, isn't it?

A big part of my focus with Steve was around his approachability factor. His team simply did not experience him as approachable. Turns out what I experienced inside our coaching sessions was very similar to what others experienced, yet no one was willing to share this feedback with Steve and it was outside of his awareness.

As we started to explore this when it showed up in the coaching sessions, Steve was able to palpably understand what was occurring in him and how it was impacting others.

FIVE TRUTHS ABOUT COURAGE

1. *Connect Heart to Heat*: The power of courage is enhanced when we use empathy. When we connect heart to heat, something happens that is otherwise impossible. There are so many ways we can exercise courage and make an observation or comment that our client is simply unable to hear and instead what shows up is defensiveness.

2. *Use What's in the Room:* Using what is right in front of us creates heat and opens the door to rapid insight because it is in the here and now. It is not a concept or an abstract notion we are talking about. This quality of immediacy creates a powerful medium for breakthrough learning.

3. *Lighten It Up:* We can invoke the wise fool or jester, the one who speaks the hard truths that no one else will utter. When we cultivate our wise fool, we are able to explore difficult issues almost in jest, so the client can hear and entertain new vantage points. A jester-like approach allows us to look together at that which is being ignored and unspoken.

4. *Stay Out of Your Client's Story:* Good boundaries keep us alert to any tendency to get drawn into our client's stories and dramas and this is how we lay the groundwork for helping the client see their stories. If we are in them, we can't help them!

5. *This Is Our Work as Coach:* This is our work, this is why leaders come to us—to see that which is invisible and to make changes that will allow them to be even more effective. When we stay out of their stories and, instead, help them see their stories and behaviors through the use of our own courage, we do our most important work as coaches.

THE COACH'S WORKSHEET: DEVELOPING MORE RANGE

Visit www.selfascoach.com for an opportunity to step back from each chapter and reflect on what meaning it has for you and what practices you might develop to keep honing your capacity as coach.

APPLYING HEAT: CASE VIGNETTE III

CASE VIGNETTE #3: RESISTANT BUT RELIABLE

You've entered into a coaching engagement with Kye. His boss has recommended this coaching because he is aware of a lot of buzz and some complaints in the system that Kye is very bristly and abrupt with others. His boss finds Kye to be exceptionally smart and able and he wants Kye to address this issue in order to continue to expand his role. Kye arrives at coaching willingly, although he is surprised this is an issue and believes it is a misperception of only a few people. You complete a round of stakeholder interviews and return to the coaching engagement reporting that this theme of bristly and abrupt (some even using the term *rude*) is widespread among all who report to him. Kye again reacts with surprise, suggesting these stakeholders are overreacting. As the coach, you are aware of feeling Kye's resistance to this input.

Coach 1

Coach 1 was worried at the contracting stage of this coaching arrangement. It was clear Kye's boss was onboard to provide the coaching and Kye seemed willing at the time but now this coach has a sense that Kye has little interest in the coaching. He finds him a bit bristly, too, and worries he will not be able to have a successful engagement with him and wishes he hadn't agreed to the work.

Where Coach 1 Is in Each of the Six Dimensions

Presence. The coach appears to be preoccupied with worries about whether or not he should have taken on this engagement and this likely degrades his ability to be fully present.

Empathy. The coach mentions that it is not easy to build a connection with Kye and we don't have enough detail to know how much of that is related to the client and how much to the coach.

Range of Feelings. The coach is aware of his own worries, but his reflections don't mention much about Kye's feelings.

Boundaries and Systems. The coach may well have good boundaries with this client, but his primary attention is focused on concerns and worries that coaching will not succeed, so there aren't sufficient reflections to allow us to observe boundaries.

Embodiment. The coach doesn't offer any comments relative to how centered or grounded he might be during the sessions.

Courage. The coach is not able to exercise courage. He does mention that Kye feels bristly to him in the coaching, but perhaps this is because he is focused on his worries or because the connection (empathy) is not strong enough; he does not share any observations or focus on "what's in the room" in the moment.

Coach 2

Coach 2 knows the coaching can always be a little trickier when it is the boss's idea, yet she finds Kye willing and believes she has built a good working alliance with him. After gathering the stakeholder input, it's clear Kye has some significant blind spots and the coach has a sense this is going to be very important for his future in the organization. She feels an urgency to dig in and help him figure out what he can change to be viewed differently, and yet, she experiences his reluctance. She resists offering her ideas about how he might make some adjustments, but she finds herself increasingly frustrated that he doesn't seem invested and doesn't seem to see how serious this might be for him.

Where Coach 2 Is in Each of the Six Dimensions

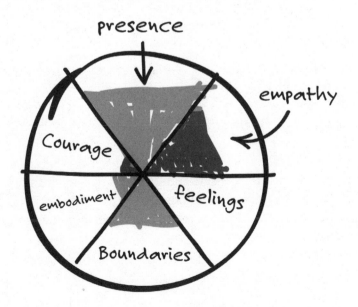

Presence. The coach appears to be fully present according to her description of what unfolds in the coaching work.

Empathy. The coach reflects on her working alliance and believes she has developed a good connectedness.

Range of Feelings. The coach seems able to fully appreciate and contain her client's feelings.

Boundaries and Systems. The coach has gathered input from the system in order to gain a wider view of what Kye's boss reports. While the coach is tempted to get into the client's story (dig in and help him), she resists, and this is a sign of some managing of boundaries in order to help the client see his situation more clearly.

Embodiment. The coach doesn't offer any reflections on how centered or grounded she feels during the coaching sessions.

Courage. The coach is able to notice and observe how the client is showing up—not as invested in making a change, not taking the feedback very seriously. However, the coach's focus on getting him onboard is a sign she is a bit drawn into her client's story. Once *in* the client's story, it is always hard to step back and use one's courage to share an observation that might be of value for the client.

Coach 3

It's clear to Coach 3 at the outset that the boss is more invested in the coaching than Kye, yet Kye is willing and so he says yes to taking on the engagement. Once he has gathered the stakeholder input, he realizes the boss might actually be underestimating the impact of Kye's behaviors and it's clear Kye is either unaware or in some denial about this. The coach decides to go slowly because it seems much of this behavior is outside of his awareness. He takes his time exploring what's working and what he feels best about and as the rapport grows, his resistance lessens and he seems interested in addressing or adjusting his behavior.

Where Coach 3 Is in Each of the Six Dimensions

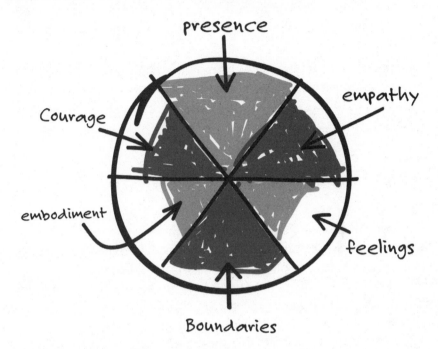

Presence. The coach seems to be fully present, managing any internal chatter attending to how his client views his situation and the stakeholder input.

Empathy. The coach reflects on his working alliance and believes he has developed a strong rapport. In addition, the coach is attuned to creating a pace that will match his client's needs as he actively continues to deepen empathy and rapport as the engagement proceeds.

Range of Feelings. The coach appears able to fully appreciate his client's feelings and his lack of awareness of the feedback he received in the stakeholder input. He notices Kye's surprise and his inclination to deny the input.

Boundaries and Systems. The coach is able to maintain strong enough boundaries to avoid any temptation to rescue or collude with Kye. This allows the coach to explore the feedback in a nonjudgmental manner that allows Kye to begin to gain awareness of these areas.

Embodiment. The coach is so present to Kye in this coaching engagement that one might guess he has some in-the-moment practices that support him in being fully centered and grounded during the sessions.

Courage. The coach is able to turn up the heat just enough to invite Kye to examine the feedback around his bristles. He mentions he is attending to timing and that is important when sharing observations or courageous transparency.

A BRIEF EPILOGUE TO THE CASE VIGNETTES

In each of these three coach approaches, I have amplified the coach's use of self in order to put a spotlight on how interconnected the six dimensions of Self as Coach are in our work. There is never one right way or a prescriptive approach to developmental coaching. The sole focus of this book is deepening one's coaching capacity by continually cultivating one's internal landscape in order to ably use self as the most important instrument in the coaching engagement.

Presence is a prerequisite to a successful engagement. The impact of unmanaged inner chatter, judgments, and assumptions is an enormous obstacle in seeing the client as they are rather than as a coach might wish them to be. Embodiment work that dependably supports a coach in getting one's self together, getting centered and grounded, supports this all-important full presence.

Empathy is fundamental in coaching. Without the ability to step into a client's shoes (without walking in them!), the engagement lacks a sense of psychological safety and trust that is needed in order to explore what's most important. Empathy is also essential when a coach uses courage in a way that may open new perspectives and new ways of seeing for the client. Courage with heart creates an invitation instead of a judgment.

Feelings are essential in coaching, as we will never change by intellectualizing or talking about a dynamic. It is in the mix of thoughts and feelings that breakthroughs occur. This means attending to feelings, noticing small signs of feelings, and staying a little longer to explore is important ground in the work of coaching.

Strong boundaries allow a coach to resist colluding and withstand the urge to don a cape and rush in to do the work for the client. When the coach has firm boundaries, they are able to more clearly observe the client's patterns and stories, and this combined with the use of courage and empathy turns up the heat for the client to see their circumstances, beliefs, or behaviors with new eyes.

Chapter 10

SUPERVISION AS A MEDIUM FOR CULTIVATING SELF AS COACH

> The real voyage of discovery consists not in seeking new
> landscapes, but in having new eyes.
>
> — *Marcel Proust*

The work of a coach is, by its very nature, insular. Whether practicing as an internal coach, as a team coach, or as a leadership coach interfacing with stakeholders, the essence of our work happens within the confines and dynamics of the coaching relationship. How do we stay alert to all that is unfolding? How do we uncover what is only vaguely emergent? How do we ask of ourselves what we ask of our clients—to observe, go deeper, risk letting go of the old, and lean into the new territories of the self?

Any good coach would agree that the quality of one's coaching is enhanced through reflective practices—the simple act of stepping back, reviewing what has transpired and asking what else might have happened, what might have been missing, and what got in the way of getting to the most important work. Yet, without a deliberate practice this can slip out of our awareness and we can rely on our old eyes instead of sharpening new ones. The tyranny of our habits, the pressure of time, and the addiction to busy-ness will inevitably prevail unless we are fully committed to turning up the heat on our own work as coach.

Coaching supervision provides this space to consciously step back and look at our work through different lenses with refreshed, sometimes new, eyes. It is here where we can deliberately focus on deepening our capacities to see, sense, hear, feel, and intuit that which lies in the margins of our awareness. This is a practice: a conscious and deliberate choice to reflect on our work in order to be at our best. Anyone who has been coaching for a time knows how universally common it is to return to a coaching session and in retrospect find oneself noticing, wondering, or perhaps worrying about what occurred at a particular moment in the session. Common reflections I have uttered myself and heard repeatedly from those in my supervision groups often sound like this:

- Something happened in the session that left me feeling uneasy.
- I felt like we didn't land on what was most important; we seemed to be talking around it.
- I was mindful of my own tenseness, sensations I'm not aware of in most coaching sessions.
- I knew I was missing an opportunity, but I was unsure in that moment of how to proceed.
- We both experienced a breakthrough moment, but I'm not sure what created it.

MY INNER LANDSCAPE: MY EARLY EXPERIENCES IN SUPERVISION

My own experiences of the power of supervision preceded the field of coaching when I was immersed in my early professional career as a clinical psychologist. In the world of psychology, supervision has long been a standard method of development at all stages of one's career. It is viewed as an essential practice in order to be at one's best; it is an ethical practice. Finding a wise and skilled supervisor is a goal and I was lucky to have the gift of working with an analytically oriented supervisor, Dr. Brams, trained and supervised by Erik Fromm in his early years. Dr. Brams was a provocative and wise analyst and supervisor. Throughout my 30s and into my 40s, I would drive out to his office regularly and explore cases and situations through new lenses. As my experience and confidence grew, I would wonder on the drive out to our session what I might learn that I wasn't capable of seeing for myself and on my return home, I would chuckle, reflecting on all I had not seen in my work, not because I lacked experience but because I am human. We will never see all there is to work with in our engagements, and we will inevitably lose track of our own stories and endless assumptions we make as people and as coaches. Expanding our view and learning to see what is hazily on the fringes is what supervision is all about. We are complicated human beings and as coaches, we are served by knowing our best reflective work is not done in isolation.

SUPERVISION PURPOSE AND MODALITIES

The reflective practice of supervision provides a medium for us to develop new ways of seeing and gain new perspectives on our work. Supervision is the term we have come to use to describe this structured practice of reflecting on our coaching work along with a trained coach supervisor equipped to support the growth and development of a coach at any stage in their career. For some of my colleagues, the term *supervision* is offputting and misleading. The term *supervisor* seems to convey for them a power dynamic and an evaluative format they find uninviting. Indeed, their reaction is understandable. The Merriam-Webster dictionary defines supervision as "the act of critically watching and directing." This definition is a far cry from the focus and purpose of the practice of coach supervision and the term does not accurately convey the essence of this powerful practice. North America was late in incorporating a structured reflective practice supporting a coach's ongoing development; other parts of the globe had already fully embraced it and termed the process supervision. Thus, for coaches in the United States, it was too late to impact the words used to describe it. So here we are—*coach supervision* it is.

ROLES OF THE COACH SUPERVISOR

The purpose of supervision aligns with the roles of the supervisor. There are several models for the supervisory roles that overlap and align. I find Erik de Haan's (2008) framework outlining three supervisory roles serves as a helpful foundation for us. His three roles include:

1. *Developer:* In this role, the supervisor provides her summary of the situation being presented along with any observations, patterns, or links she makes to what is being presented. The focus in this role is solely on the coach's development.
2. *Gatekeeper:* In this role, the supervisor views it as their responsibility to be the gatekeeper for the profession of coaching and in those rare situations where ethical boundaries are not heeded or the coach's approach is outside the parameters of coaching, the supervisor makes this known to the coach and together they develop a course of action that protects the client, the profession, and ultimately, the coach going forward.
3. *Nurse:* In this role, the supervisor works to create a restorative space for the coach through creation of a safe space that emphasizes encouraging and approachable interventions that allow the coach to grow, thrive, and stretch their capacity.

FORMATS FOR SUPERVISION

In addition to purpose and roles in supervision, there are several common formats for this work, each having some unique qualities, advantages, and potential downsides.

Group Supervision

This is a format that typically includes a supervisor along with four to six coach supervisees meeting monthly for a 90- to 120-minute session. On occasions when in-person sessions are possible, that is ideal; but most often this occurs via web video calls allowing group members to see one another onscreen during the course of each call. Coach supervisees use the time to discuss a part of their coaching work, a pattern or theme they are noticing, or something unique to themselves as related to the coaching work. This format allows for a combination of work with the supervisor, insights and observations from other group members, and links to common ground uncovered for all in the course of any of the discussions that ensue. The coach supervisee might bring to supervision a moment in a session, a transcript of a portion of a session, a recording of a portion of a session, a written free-association of a session, or any other format that proves helpful to the coach. The group interaction brings richness to the supervision and allows members to learn from another's case or challenge as well as from their own situations. The drawback for some is there is less time for 1:1 focus and that is sometimes an important consideration for the coach.

Individual Supervision

This format is highly personalized with a 1:1 approach. All that occurs in group supervision occurs in 1:1, with an individualized focus between coach and supervisor. The drawback for some is there is not an opportunity to gain input and insights from other colleagues nor is there the opportunity to learn from the cases and challenges from others.

Peer Supervision

This approach can be a preferred alternative for coaches with substantial experience in supervision and perhaps as coach supervisors. It is also commonly recommended in group supervision that the group meets once each month as a peer group in addition to the supervisor-led monthly call. It's also common for those coaches experienced in supervision to engage solely in peer supervision.

Inner Supervisor

This approach is one we can all draw upon at times and, in fact, engaging our *inner supervisor* is a powerful tool we can invoke for our own development at all times.

There are a variety of models and approaches to coach supervision referenced later in this chapter, and given that the original sources are well known and widely available, my primary focus in this chapter is on cultivating the inner supervisor and directing the reader to additional sources for in-depth perspectives.

FROM MY INNER LANDSCAPE: MY CURRENT EXPERIENCES IN SUPERVISION

Today, as an experienced coach and coach supervisor, I regularly engage in all forms of supervision from my inner supervisor to group supervision, knowing my work is always enhanced when I actively reflect in the company of a coach supervisor who inevitably sees that which is only dimly visible to me. Like most coaches, I have two or three areas of self that fall into the "dimly visible" category, and when a light is shined on one of these areas, my work is stronger and my development deeper. One of these areas in my work, a never-ending aspect of my development, is cultivating more heart and, in so doing, demonstrating more vulnerability. What I have come to refer to as my "be strong" story was a smart one to devise as a child, but as an adult, a parent, a coach, and a leader, it has long been evident to me that it has a downside in equal portions to the upside. It has been an area of development I have worked on most of my adult life and will likely continue to work on forever. Here's how it showed up not long ago in a supervision session I was having with a superb coach supervisor.

I brought a situation to 1:1 supervision, a small segment of a supervision session that I knew could have gone differently. Even in the moment I was aware that more could have unfolded if I had just been a little more alert to how I might more skillfully pivot. The segment of the supervision session went like this:

> The coach brought a case to our call and as he described his client and his own stance with the client I was aware in the moment that I was managing a reaction I was having, which was something like, "That sounds like a wild thing." I focused on my judgment and reaction and worked to put them on the shelf and manage myself to simply be present in the moment. While I knew sharing my judgment would be wholly unhelpful, I was confident I missed an opportunity to explore something important in that moment. I was aware, or at least I imagined, that others in the group were also holding back a bit, as the group remained nearly silent and even when I queried others about what was happening, very little was forthcoming.

As I described this vignette to my supervisor, she made three observations and comments that threaded through our discussion:

1. She wondered what might have emerged if I had consciously paused to center myself with a breath, activated my heart, and then magnified the moment.
2. She wondered how I might explicitly put more space around a moment like this, sharing more of what's happening in myself in a heartful way and wondering how it was for the other?
3. Then, after we had explored both of these powerful inquiries and as we neared the end of the session, she wondered, "In your life right now, what might change for you to be just a bit more heartful with yourself?"

These were powerful observations and inquiries and all delivered with lightness and heart. She was drawing my attention to my work—cultivating more heart. This will always be a part of my work. Today, after many years of my work as a coach supervisor, I regularly ask myself, "If I had come from more heart, what might have unfolded differently?" Today, as a human being, I return to the wonderful question, "If I were to magnify an open heart in my private life, what might emerge in new ways?"

If we return to the roots of our stories and essence of our beliefs and how we develop as leaders and coaches, all that we have recounted in our own supervision and development links to honing a twice-born life—going vertical in our development, building the capacity to turn subject into object, and staying awake to the stories that could lead us to live half awake, in habit instead of in choice.

"WHO YOU ARE IS HOW YOU COACH"

Coach supervision first emerged in Western Europe and in the United Kingdom, in particular. The roots of the terminology and the practice are well documented in the field of psychology as a means of continually deepening one's capacity. Edna Murdoch, one of the early pioneers in coach supervision emanating from the United Kingdom, often uses this wonderful phrase: Who you are is how you coach. Edna credits Aboodi Shabi as first saying this to her, but I believe she is responsible for implanting this powerful message in the work of so many of us. It's piercing to consider the meaning of these seven words. Who you are is how you coach. It suggests that knowing who we are as coaches is a requirement if we are going to do our best work. It suggests that understanding the origins of our stories and beliefs is essential in having a perspective that is agile. It suggests that to be a great coach demands much of us, and the practice of coaching supervision adds a potent platform to cultivate our Self as Coach and our capacity to be great.

At Hudson, we established the first Coach Supervision Center in the United States in 2012, as a small group of master coaches who had been engaged in a year-long coach supervision training experience in London. Upon completion of our own supervision training experience, we began offering group supervision to leaders completing our year-long coach certification program. No matter how high the quality of a coach certification program or an academic degree program might be, the work of becoming a great coach requires practice, reflection, input, and adjustments throughout the course of a coach's life cycle. In our Supervision Center, we have found the impact of group supervision to be especially meaningful for coaches committed to being at their best through their own development.

THE INNER SUPERVISOR IN YOU

Admittedly, I have a bias that coaches support their own development and their best work with clients by engaging in regular supervision and at this time in this young field of coaching, we have a growing body of literature supporting this position. Today, in the field of coaching, supervision models and processes are well established and powerful sources of learning and guidance for us. While I will briefly review a few of the well-known models and approaches, my bigger goal is to broadly make linkages that will entice you, the coach, to explore these sources in more depth as you develop your own inner supervisor. Structured supervision will always play an important role in our work as coaches, yet equally important is our commitment to developing practices to examine our work in new ways with new eyes and to continually engage in a disciplined reflective process that turns up the heat on our work.

OUR INNER SUPERVISOR SUPPORTS OUR VERTICAL DEVELOPMENT

When we ask bigger questions about our work, when we step back to deeply pause and notice that which is on the fringes of our work, when we pay attention to what scared us and what left us feeling uneasy, we are taking a deeper dive. When we enlarge our awareness of what is happening inside us as coach—our breath, pace, tensions, and how we hold ourselves—and draw our attention to the dynamics happening between coach and client, we are focused on our vertical development. The emphasis is much less on "what should I do?" with supervisees coming to seek answers and direction. This is not a space for the supervisor to play the role of "if I were you," which is so tempting for many of us. Rather, this space is a mighty challenge to go deeper instead of riding the surface of our favorite "tells"!

On the surface, it seems satisfying to seek the answers from others and search for tools that might help, and while these are useful and have a place in our work, the supervision space and the inner supervisor work encourages and provides an opportunity to step back and reflect on what happened in a particular session or a series of sessions, what didn't happen, what was happening for the coach, what was missed, what was aroused by the work, what was attended to, and what was ignored. These explorations lead to the cultivation of new territory and depths for the coach; these explorations expand our work. Imagine asking yourself some of the following questions after each of your coaching sessions.

BIGGER QUESTIONS TO CULTIVATE YOUR INNER SUPERVISOR AND DEEPEN YOUR WORK

As you read the list below, you will see the interplay of the Self as Coach dimensions at work as you ask yourself these questions and hone your inner supervisor:

- How did I show up for this session?
- Was I present and centered or scrambled and wobbly?
- What feelings and thoughts were present as I walked into this session with this particular client?

- Was I able to arrive with a fresh set of eyes?
- How did my client show up?
- How did our session begin?
- What were the opening words?
- What was my intention?
- What did I notice about my own inner rumblings – my biases, hopes, concerns?
- What were my client's requests and hopes for our time together in this session?
- How might I describe the quality of our holonic energy?
- How would I describe my working alliance with my client?
- Are there any ways I might adjust my empathy—too much, too little?
- What signals occurred that gave me a sense my client feels connected?
- How was my own boundary management? Was I able to help my client see their story or circumstances instead of allowing myself to get drawn into the situation?
- Was I aware of any urge to rescue my client?
- Is there anything this client stirs in me? Is there anyone this client reminds me of?
- Are there interventions I felt particularly useful?
- Are there observations that I did not share?
- Were there times in the session when I had a sense there was something else I might do or be but couldn't find the entry or the courage? What can I learn from this?
- Was I attuned to the broader environment of my client as we worked?
- How did our session conclude?
- What is important for me to remember and ponder before our next session?
- What are the emerging stories and stances my client lives and only sees dimly?
- Is there anything that makes me uneasy or uncomfortable in the presence of this particular client?
- What didn't I say or do that might have proven useful in this session?

HAVEN AND HARBOR

Supervision—whether formally undertaken in group or individual work, or when cultivating your inner supervisor—is a haven and a harbor wherein a coach is able to take a step back and look at their work from a variety of angles, seeking to gain new views. This space allows a coach to deepen their capacity to use what's in the room, create heat experiences, understand one's own stories, question one's beliefs, delve into one's vertical development, and uncover new edges of development. This is the haven where a coach is able to speak the unsayable, admit the unthinkable, take risks that feel uncomfortable, safely explore, then awaken to one's own limiting stories, seeing and sensing in new ways the dimensions of one's Self as Coach.

Supervision is a place focused on the now rather than the space in which we talk about, theorize, or plan. The supervision experience often parallels what has unfolded in coaching as well as what has unfolded in the vignettes brought to supervision. When we are able to see parallels, new doors open for us. There are a handful of discoveries we can uncover with just a few key inquiries like the following:

- As you scan your coaching engagements, what do you notice about your approach, your habits, your go-to models and tools. Even while these approaches and tools may bring value, how might they cause you to miss something? Might your regular approaches and tools leave you overlooking small signals that might bear fruit?
- As you scan your development as a coach, where have your growth spurts come from and what have these growth spurts uncovered for you in your coaching? Could you graph the pivots or draw a picture that captures them?
- Most often, our learning comes from the tough times, the unknowns, and the ones that keep us up at night. Spend some time capturing the list of your tough times over the past year. See if, upon reflection, you are able to discern key themes that are useful.

There are helpful models and frameworks in the field of coaching that are particularly useful in traditional supervision and in cultivating one's inner supervisor. The details of these models are readily available for any coach to explore so, for the purposes of this book, I will mention the most prominent models and seek to link them, highlighting both common ground and distinctive features.

FRAMEWORKS AND MODELS TO GROW YOUR INNER SUPERVISOR

This brief review of some key frameworks and models, used in traditional supervision and helpful in growing your inner supervisor, is meant to whet your appetite and encourage you to explore in more detail. I begin with two models on reflective practices that then inform the other models in this section.

Schön's Teachings on Reflective Practices

It's impossible to review models of supervision that highlight reflective practices without recognizing Donald Schön's (1987) early work on supervision in PhD coaching. In the early 1980s, he was already examining how we learn, and his explorations led him to believe that the only learning that has the capacity to deeply influence one's behavior comes from self-discovery, stimulated by a coach's ability to help someone learn what is important for them, rather than teach someone else what you deem essential.

Argyris and Schön's Double Loop Learning

Chris Argyris and Donald Schön, in *Organizational Learning: A Theory of Action Perspective* (1978), debuted double-loop learning, which has become a widely used model for learning. The most common approach to learning was once single-loop-focused on looking at results and problem-solving to improve on those results. Double-loop learning, shown in Figure 10.1, challenged leaders to go a step well beyond fixing or improving upon a problem and, instead, asked leaders to go deeper and challenge underlying assumptions and beliefs that dictate and determine what we do.

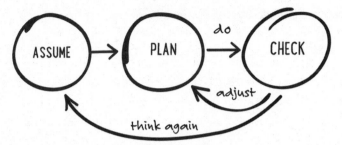

Figure 10.1 Argyris and Schön's Double-Loop Learning

Self as Coach Model

The Self as Coach model (Figure 10.2) provides ample ground for amplifying awareness using each of the domains. Throughout this book, I have offered reflective inquiries you might use to amplify your awareness of your capacity to use *self* in your work.

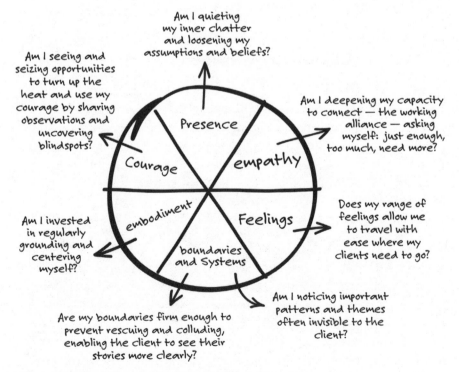

Figure 10.2 Self as Coach: Sample Reflective Inquiries

Hawkin's Seven-Eyed Process Model

Peter Hawkins (2007) developed a thoroughly useable model for coach supervision that has deftly stood the test of time. His studies reveal that each supervisor seemed to have a consistent area of focus in their supervision work and that focus, more than any other factor, was responsible for their styles. This led to an awareness that there are several key areas of focus essential in supervision; hence, the seven-eyed process model of supervision emerged and continues to evolve into its present form for use in coaching supervision today. The current model reflects the work and collaborative thinking of Hawkins along with Smith, Schwenk, and Shohet. It also draws on the work of de Haan as it relates to the internal and relational lives of individuals.

The seven-eyed process model (Figure 10.3) includes seven foci for exploring a coaching session, including: (1) the client; (2) interventions chosen by the coach; (3) coach and client relationship; (4) the coach; (5) coach and supervisor relationship; (6) supervisor focus on one's own process; and (7) the wider context of the engagement.

Clutterbuck's Seven Conversations

Clutterbuck (2010) created the seven conversations model shown in Figure 10.4 to draw the coach's (and coach supervisor's) attention to all that occurs in a coaching engagement beyond the specific dialogue during the coaching sessions. He sought to enlarge the coach's perspective beyond what the coach did or said in the session by highlighting dialogue between and within coach and client. In so doing, he emphasized

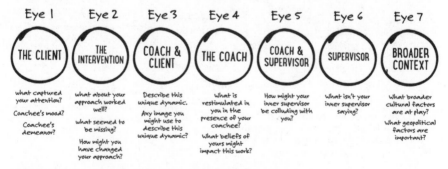

Figure 10.3   Hawkins Seven-Eyed Process Model of Supervision

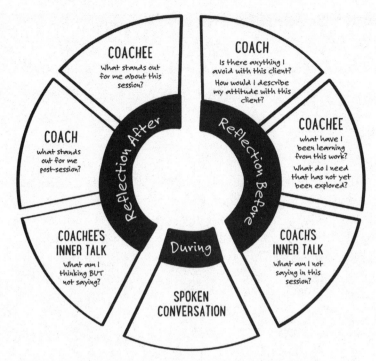

Figure 10.4 Clutterbuck's Seven Conversations in Supervision

a systemic view of dialogic dynamics. He stresses that the spoken dialogue that occurs in a coaching session is highly dependent on the other conversations, the internal and contextual preparation the coach engages in prior to the session, as well the client's internal conversations and preparation.

These models provide maps to guide our reflections into areas we might miss or avoid. Each map has a slightly different focus with plenty of overlapping and linked territory. Don't land on just one; try all of these and more. Our reflective practices need to be disrupted in order that we might stay fully awake, lean into new areas of our development, and risk letting go of well-worn habits that don't serve us as well today as they may have in the past.

DEEPENING YOUR IMPACT: EXPLORE COMMON DYNAMICS IN SUPERVISION

There are three common dynamics in supervision worth exploring. Work through some of the reflective questions for each of the following dynamics.

Countertransference

Countertransference occurs when the coach transfers past experiences onto the client (or in supervision, the supervisor transfers past experiences onto the supervisee). This happens due to what is aroused in the coach in response to the client.

- What has been triggered in me in the presence of this coachee?

- Where and what might this be connected to from my past?

- How can I use this in our work to serve my coachee or manage it in order to be fully present?

- Does this coachee remind me of anyone?

- Were there unique feelings aroused in me in the presence of this particular coachee?

Psychological Contract

The psychological contract between coach and client or coach and coach supervisor is the nearly invisible and unspoken agreement that shows up as the work evolves in those situations where the coach doesn't take time early in the work to fully explore this.

- What aren't we talking about as we launch this coaching?

- What is not being said that might get in our way further down the road?

- What might you be hoping for that we have not explored?

Parallel Process

A parallel process occurs when a dynamic in a relationship is repeated at other levels. In supervision or with our inner supervisor, the parallel process can be either a quagmire or an opportunity. The key is in being present to recognize this is occurring.

- As you describe this situation is there anything about it that is familiar to you?

- Have you experienced this dynamic before?

- Is this situation new or do you know something about it from your past?

SUPERVISION AS THE ETHICAL COMPASS FOR SELF AS COACH

Supervision widens our view of who we are as coach and allows us to gain a clearer view of what lurks in the shadows and limits our work. To be great leadership coaches we need to be steadily and regularly immersed in our own development. Development takes time, practice, and reflection in order to create deep change at the vertical level rather than clinging to what to do and the tools to employ.

Chapter 11

SELF AS LEADER

> Great leaders ponder the question of what they would like
> to leave behind as a legacy in life. How do we want to be
> remembered? I believe true leaders take the kinds of actions
> that will benefit the next generation.
> — *Manfred Kets de Vries*

SELF-AWARE LEADERS

"This work has changed how I am as a leader. For so long I thought I don't have time for the 'soft stuff,' and now I realize this is actually the most important stuff that makes all of the hard stuff work."

I will long remember these words from a senior physician leader in a large health-care system. These words were communicated following an intensive coach training program our organization led where we focused on coaching, going deeper, and examining the internal landscape of the leader. His eyes moistened as he shared the impact the training had for him. I had observed how present and engaged he was throughout the five-month learning journey, so I asked him if we could sit and talk a bit so I could learn more about how his leadership had changed. Like so many other leaders, he has a tough role in a large and ever-changing industry and the manner in which he leads, shows up, and manages himself impacts hundreds of people within his unit.

Much like the remarks of this dedicated physician leader, the leaders we work with, whether in a coaching engagement or a coach training experience, are seeking ways to be at their best as they navigate the daily challenges in their roles. In the end, the concept of starting at home, going deeper internally, and using the Self as Coach model as a framework for exploring blind spots and unknown territory resonates and proves equally relevant in the life of a leader. The following are the themes I took from our conversation.

Listening with new ears. He told me of several stories wherein he *thought he knew* until he started listening with what he termed his *new ears,* which meant listening for what he might not know instead of his old style of "I've heard this before" or "yep, this sounds familiar." He repeatedly told me how surprised he was about what was really going on with his people, what was challenging for them that he had not recognized, and what they needed from him that he was unaware of in the past.

This reminded me of Chris Argyris's well-known model of the Ladder of Inference (1990). In his model (Figure 11.1), our old ears rapidly drive us up the ladder—choosing only some data, making assumptions, supporting our beliefs, and taking action in a matter of seconds. Over time, his research found that the longer one has been in a leadership role, the faster the climb up the ladder of inference and the more likely the "I've seen this one before" style prevails. Listening with new ears is akin to walking oneself back down the ladder and

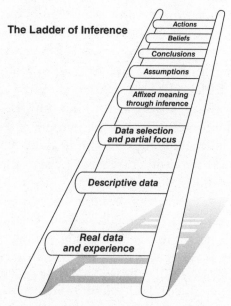

The Ladder of Inference

Actions
Beliefs
Conclusions
Assumptions
Affixed meaning through inference
Data selection and partial focus
Descriptive data
Real data and experience

Figure 11.1   Argyris's Ladder of Inference

staying curious about what is happening for the other, managing the urge to make assumptions, and practicing the art of being fully present to another in order to be surprised and to learn.

Asking far more than telling. The physician leader shared with me that one of the toughest and most transformative adjustments he has made in his approach is an intentional daily practice of asking his people more than telling them. He laughed as he shared how hard something that sounds so simple actually is and admitted that he long believed his greatest value was in providing his answers and in telling others how to proceed. When he asks, he learns what others need most, where their obstacles are, and what they might be wanting from him in that moment. Asking also creates the grounds for more trust, empathy, connection, and fuller understanding of another person.

Edgar Schein's recent works, *Humble Inquiry: The Gentle Art of Asking Instead of Telling* (2013) and *Humble Leadership: The Power of Relationships, Openness, and Trust* (2018), underlines the power of asking. He writes these powerful words in *Humble Inquiry*:

> We take it for granted that telling is more valued than asking. Asking the right questions is valued, but asking in general is not. To ask is to reveal ignorance and weakness. Knowing things is highly valued, and telling people what we know is almost automatic because we have made it habitual in most situations.

Schein's words underline what a tough and important challenge it is for today's leaders to consciously make the pivot from telling to asking.

Reflecting regularly changes me. The physician leader also admitted that he initially resisted the reflective practices we engaged in during the program and balked at our encouragement to build even a small reflective practice because it didn't seem like something he could make a priority in his busy work day. But, being a good sport while in the program, he tried it on and he was surprised at what unfolded for him. He began to notice what he had been avoiding and what had been keeping him up at night. Interestingly enough, these things were most often in the interpersonal domain—the tough conversations and feedback he was avoiding or the frustrations he was experiencing with a key member or two of his team.

"Getting on the balcony" is how Heifetz and Linsky (2009), authors of *The Practice of Adaptive Leadership*, describe the capacity to step back and gain a broader, higher level view of what is occurring in the moment. They describe it in this way:

Taking a balcony perspective is extremely tough to do when you are fiercely engaged down below being pushed and pulled by the events and people around you. The process of stepping back . . . enables you to observe your own actions and see yourself objectively . . . perhaps the hardest task of all.

This practice of getting on the balcony is a reflection in the moment that provides a sharper view of self and others.

Seeking feedback from others. The physician leader confessed that he had stopped asking for feedback from members of his team and those working closely with him and had come to rely on his own perceptions as his most reliable ones. While in the program, he realized he was missing some valuable input that could enable him to be a better leader of his people. While he was still early in the process of seeking feedback, he had already engaged in three informal conversations with members of his senior team; he was surprised by some of their input and knew that was a sign he needed to seek it out from others and continue to do so more often.

Tasha Eurich's book, *Insight: The Surprising Truth About How Others See Us, How We See Ourselves, and Why the Answers Matter More Than We Think* (2018), highlights this theme of self-awareness relative to seeking feedback. Eurich characterizes this self-awareness as the "meta-skill of the twenty-first century" (2018). Her research debunks the notion that introspection alone produces self-awareness and she distinguishes between two categories of self-awareness: *internal* and *external*. External self-awareness is knowing how others see and experience you. She writes "to be truly self-aware, we must . . . understand our impact: that is, how our behavior affects others" (Eurich, 2018). The cost of being oblivious to one's impact on their teams is predictable and Eurich puts a spotlight on this when she writes, "Leaders who lack self-awareness bring down team performance, reduce decision quality by an average of 36 percent, hurt coordination by 46% and increase conflict by 30%" (2018).

The act of regularly seeking feedback is a differentiator for a leader but it's not always easy to gain straight talk from others. Manfred Kets de Vries (2014) reminds us that often leaders encircle themselves with friends or long-time colleagues who don't challenge or disagree with them. As he provocatively puts it, "They are surrounded by walls, mirrors and liars." So, seeking feedback requires courage: the courage to ask and ask often and the courage to ask those who will speak truth to power.

These threads of the work of others on leadership and my own work on Self as Coach came together in my mind in my conversation with this humble physician leader who had simply observed, ". . . the soft stuff makes the hard stuff possible!" His lessons and the ways in which his leadership has changed through the vertical development experience of our work together touched on all areas of the Self as Coach model we have examined.

The dimensions I link to Self as Coach are also at play for every leader-coachee at any level as they cultivate their internal landscape in an effort to be at their best.

The work of a great coach is to facilitate changes and unlock new layers of potential in others in ways that matter to the individual and the systems in which they work. The most predictable, teachable, transferable elements of a traditional coaching approach are found in skill-based competencies, a reliable methodology, and tools and resources unique and relevant to a leadership coach. The less predictable element that is a significant differentiator is found in the deeper work of cultivating one's internal landscape — Self as Coach — in order to use one's self as the most important instrument in the work. Chapters 3 through 9 have been a kind of roadmap for the unexplored and unpredictable terrain of Self as Coach, but the question remains: How do coaches guide leaders into the similarly uncharted territory of Self as Leader? How does self-awareness and ease with examining one's internal landscape benefit a leader?

While the work of a leader is much broader in scope and the scope grows as the leader rises, the ability to explore the inner terrain of self may be one of the most important instruments in leading others and unlocking new layers of potential in those one leads. Throughout the leadership lifecycle, this is a differentiator at each step along the path. This capacity becomes increasingly important as one moves up the leadership ladder, and as roles grow in scope and responsibilities have the power to impact broader swathes of the culture and multiple layers of leaders in the organization. The technical skills that were critical earlier in one's career are now eclipsed by the importance of a depth of self-awareness that allows a leader to effectively lead and inspire others.

Over two decades ago, Daniel Goleman (1995) was writing about the importance of self-awareness in the life of a leader at any level in the organization. He wrote, "Emotional intelligence is the *sine qua non* of leadership, without it, a person can have the best training, the sharpest analytical mind and endless smart ideas, yet be unable to be a great leader." Bill George and Doug Baker's (2011) research on authentic leadership asked 75 members of Stanford's Business Advisory Council about the most important capability leaders need to cultivate. Their nearly unanimous response concurred with Goleman's long-held position—it is *self-awareness*.

SELF AS COACH DIMENSIONS ARE ALSO SELF AS LEADER DIMENSIONS

Several elements of the Self as Coach dimensions are most relevant for *self as leader* in deepening self-awareness, including: presence, empathy, courage, and systemic thinking.

Presence. The leader whose presence is an intervention is a leader able to fully focus on what's most important in the moment and consciously manage to put other conversations and priorities in the background. The leader who is routinely inaccessible, always in a rush, and multitasking sends just that message to those on the team. A leader's presence plays a critical role in the culture of their team and the wider organization.

Empathy. The leader able to exercise just the right degree of empathy builds psychological safety and trust that allows others to openly share what's often lurking below the surface and creating obstacles at other levels. The use of empathy for a leader has more layers than for the coach. Empathy builds trust and safety and the leader who is able to demonstrate their own vulnerability will create a stronger empathic connection. According to sociologist Brene Brown (2012), vulnerability builds trust and elevates performance for leaders.

Courage. The leader with courage is one whom others want to follow. This kind of leader has the courage to step into the fire when it matters most, have tough conversations, and offer feedback and perspectives in the service of the other, the team, and the organization. Master coach and author, Mary Beth O'Neill (2007) often writes about the powerful combination of backbone and heart. A leader needs both to be effective, and backbone requires courage.

Systemic Thinking. The leader at any level needs to embrace systemic thinking in order to be at their best, from the system inside a small team to the overall system of the organization. Peter Senge, in *The Fifth Discipline*, wrote, "Systemic thinking is a discipline of seeing the whole. It is a framework for seeing interrelationships rather than things, seeing patterns of change rather than static snapshots" (1990). Seeing patterns instead of discrete events, recognizing the whole instead of a segment, thinking systemically rather than individualistically—this is the discipline that supports great leadership.

Turning up the heat in order to support development and change is as important for the leader as it is for the coach. It's part of a leader's job, and the model of Self as Coach provides the conditions for a leader to learn to create heat.

PURPOSE-DRIVEN LEADERS

The Global Leadership Forecast (2018) is a three-way collaborative research project conducted by Ernst & Young Global Limited, Development Dimensions International, and The Conference Board. It integrates research data from over 25,000 leaders across 2,500 organizations spanning more than 1,000 C-Suite executives from over 50 countries representing 25 major industries. The forecast's findings indicate that at the top of the agenda of concerns for today's CEOs is the ability to develop and advance leaders at all levels in order to stay ahead of the growing complexities of the business landscape. These are concerns for which current approaches in coaching are woefully insufficient. Another theme emerging from the forecast is the power of purpose-driven leaders and organizations. According to the findings of the 2018 forecast, there is a "growing body of evidence demonstrating that a strong and active purpose raises employee engagement, acts as a unifier, makes customers more committed and builds organizational resilience." The forecast goes on to say that "real benefits come when leaders 'walk the walk' by behaving in a manner that exemplifies their organization's purpose" (Ernst & Young Global Limited, Development Dimensions International, and The Conference Board, 2018).

Leaders who walk the walk are aligned to a bigger mission. The study finds that purposeful organizations enjoy some of important benefits that mirror much of what has been explored in previous chapters including:

- Stronger culture
- Higher levels of psychological safety
- More resilience
- Regular feedback and a culture where "radical candor" prevails
- A track record of investing in coaching, mentoring, and learning from one another—leader to leader

Whether coach, leader, or organization, we need an overarching sense of purpose, a North Star that inspires greatness and aligns with our values. For the coach, the North Star is the aspirational goal of those with whom they work. For the leader, the North Star is the vision and purpose of the organization and team they are serving. When our North Star is clear and visible, our work as coach or leader is aligned with clarity, and our ability to communicate this regularly and clearly inspires others to follow a leader. Presence to the ecology of the broader system, awareness of systems at all levels, and courage to continually live by and communicate purpose is fundamental for leaders today.

LEADER'S USE OF THE INNER SUPERVISOR

Our VUCA world is a given, but the choice to step into the twice-born space that emerges when cultivating self-awareness and one's internal landscape is one that is a true differentiator. Today's leaders are faced with challenges that history does not adequately inform nor do leadership books and competencies adequately address, but what we do know is that self-awareness—awareness of one's internal landscape with all of the stories, stances, assumptions, and biases at play—is a differentiator.

Gone are the days of believing leaders are born as such, that charisma is key, and that hierarchical leadership is king or queen. Today's abundance of current research and writing on leadership points us in the direction of authenticity, self-awareness, humility, agility, courage, and more; and all of these characteristics require leaders to be able to understand their own stories, their internal landscape, and all that lies beneath the surface. Just as this is true for a master executive or leadership coach, the leader who is able to peer at one's self through the lenses of Horney, Bowlby, Kegan, and others is a human being willing to unearth stories and stances that may be informative and often worthy of dismantling in order to reconstruct parts of one's past or current self in order to meet the challenges of the future.

Leaders who possess the wisdom and courage to seek feedback often and at several levels are leaders who are willing to be vulnerable, expose their blind spots, and, in so doing, cultivate an inner supervisor. The inner supervisor of the leader is the voice that whispers,

- *Step back, take a broader view, and notice what might be missing in you before others (presence).*
- *Pause, slow your pace, and learn by asking more and knowing less (empathy).*
- *Take care of yourself so you are able to be there for your people (empathy).*
- *Don't wear a cape; enable and grow others instead of taking it on yourself (boundaries and systems).*
- *Be courageous; your people need your courage (courage).*
- *Practice humility; it creates safety and builds trust (presence).*
- *Turn up the heat when it makes a difference; people want to grow (courage).*

THE INNER WORK OF SELF AS LEADER

Scattered throughout this book, I have included my inner reflections in order to provide a glimpse into how I have put conceptual material to work for myself. We learn through reflection, practice, and reflection again. This is true for a coach, a leader, and all of us as human beings. Reflection or a reflective practice needn't take much time, but it does require a discipline, a practice that supports our return to it repeatedly—that's how we grow and change. The inner work of a leader may have a focus that is more dispersed and multilayered than a coach by virtue of their role.

LEADERSHIP LESSONS FROM PATAGONIA: A LEADER WHO HAS TURNED UP THE HEAT TO MAKE A DIFFERENCE

Just down the road from our offices in Santa Barbara is a company, a founder, and leaders demonstrating these much-needed dimensions. The company is Patagonia, and its humble visionary has lived by the commitments of knowing one's self and taking actions that will benefit the next generation. Founded by Yvon Chouinard, the mission is simple: "Build the best product, cause no unnecessary harm, use business to inspire and implement solutions to the environmental crisis." Since the early 1980s, Patagonia has made environmental responsibility an important part of everyone's work at the company. They use recycled paper in their catalogs, recycled polyester in their fleece products, and recycled products in their distribution centers ranging from rebar, carpets, retrofitted lighting systems, and more. Chouinard and his company live up to their mission, and their values model the way for others.

The rudder of purpose that drives a company's mission is a game changer, and self-awareness fuels what is possible in the organization. Chouinard is a leader who demonstrates both a purpose-driven mission and self-awareness. In his book, *Let My People Go Surfing: The Education of a Reluctant Businessman* (2005), Chouinard wrote, "You have to be true to yourself; you have to know strengths and limitations and live within your means." He cultivated a culture at Patagonia that values their mission, views work-life balance as essential, and inspires the best in others through his empathy, ability to listen, and a true passion for the work and the mission of the company.

Patagonia has the advantage of being a privately held company largely immune to the board's attention to quarterly stock performance and shareholder value. It also has the distinct advantage of a long run by a mission-driven founder who is, even now, continuing to guide at a high level as he steps away from the day-to-day operations.

There are lessons we can take from Patagonia and others like it who have embraced clear missions and emotionally intelligent leadership. A clear mission matters, making a difference in the world inspires, and to return to the message of this book, a leader who has honed his or her self-awareness is someone others want to follow.

Old habits, stories, and beliefs left unattended will drive us, and the work of self as leader is a vertical domain requiring commitment, regular practices, collegial support, and feedback. The words of the physician leader are worth remembering: The soft stuff is actually the hardest stuff! Whether a leader or a leadership coach, the baseline competencies and skills are essential, and are often the price of entry into a field, but what we often term *the soft stuff* of emotional intelligence, knowing one's self, continuously cultivating one's internal landscape—this is what makes a great leader or leadership coach.

REFERENCES

Ainsworth, M.D.S., & Bowlby, J. (1991). An ethological approach to personality development. *American Psychologist, 46,* 331–341.

Argyris, C. (1990). *Overcoming organizational defenses: Facilitating organizational learning.* New York: Pearson.

Argyris, C., & Schön, D. (1978). *Organizational learning: A theory of action perspective.* Reading, MA: Addison Wesley.

Arnold, J., & Murdoch, E. (2013). *Full Spectrum Supervision: Who You are is How You Supervise.* London, UK: Panoma Press Ltd.

Batson, C.D. (2009). These things called empathy: Eight related but distinct phenomena. In J. Decety & W. Ickes (Eds.), *Social neuroscience. The social neuroscience of empathy* (pp. 3–15). Cambridge, MA: MIT Press.

Bowen, M. (1985). *Family therapy in clinical practice.* Lanham, MD: Rowman & Littlefield.

Bowlby J. (1973). *Separation: Anxiety and anger, attachment and loss* (Vol. II). New York: Basic Books.

Breeze, C.G., & Dehungara, K. (2011). The Challenger Spirit. London, UK: LID Publishing Inc.

Brown, B. (2012). *Daring greatly: How the courage to be vulnerable transforms the way we live, love, parent, and lead.* New York: Penguin.

Chandler, D.E., & Kram, K.E. (2005). Applying an adult development perspective to developmental network. *Career Development International, 10*(6/7), 548–566.

Chouinard, Y. (2005). *Let my people go surfing: The education of a reluctant businessman—including 10 more years of business unusual.* New York: Penguin.

Clutterbuck, D. (2011, June). *Using the seven conversations in supervision.* Presentation to the First Annual Coach Supervision Conference, Oxford University, Oxford, UK.

de Haan, E. (2008). *Relational coaching: Journeys towards mastering one-to-one learning*. San Francisco: Wiley.

Damasio, A.R. (1994). *Descartes' error: Emotion, reason and the human brain*. New York: Random House.

Ernst & Young Global Limited, Development Dimensions International, and The Conference Board. (2018). *Global Leadership Forecast 2018*. Retrieved from https://www.ddiworld.com/DDI/media/trend-research/glf2018/global-leadership-forecast-2018_ddi_tr.pdf?ext=.pdf

Eurich, T. (2018). *Insight: The surprising truth about how others see us, how we see ourselves, and why the answers matter more than we think*. New York: Random House.

Feldman Barrett, L. (2018). *How emotions are made*. New York: Mariner Books.

Fridjhon, M., & Fuller, F. (2013). An introduction to relationship systems intelligence [White Paper]. CRR Global. Retrieved from http://www.teamcoachingzone.com/wp-content/uploads/2015/01/RSI-White-Paper.pdf

Gallwey, T. (1974). *The inner game of tennis*. New York: Random House.

George, B., & Baker, D. (2011). *True North groups: A powerful path to personal and leadership development*. San Francisco: Berrett-Koehler.

Goleman, D. (1995). *Emotional intelligence*. New York: Bantam Books.

Hamill, P. (2013). *Embodied leadership: The somatic approach to developing your leadership*. London: Kogan Page Ltd.

Hawkins, P. (2017). *Leadership team coaching: Developing collective transformational leadership* (3rd ed.). London: Kogan Page Ltd.

Hawkins, P. (2018). Resourcing: The neglected third leg of supervision. In E. Turner & S. Palmer (Eds.), *The heart of supervision*. London: Routledge.

Hawkins, P., & Smith, N. (2007). *Coaching, mentoring and organizational consultancy*. Berkshire, England: Open University Press.

Hawkins, P., & Smith, N. (2013). *Coaching, mentoring and organizational consultancy: Supervision and development* (2nd ed.). Maidenhead: Open University Press/McGraw Hill.

Hawkins, P., & Turner, E. (2017). The rise of coaching supervision. *International Journal of Coaching, 10* (2), 102–104. Retrieved from http://dx.doi.org/10.1080/17521882.2016.1266002

Heifetz, R., & Linsky, M. (2009). *The practice of adaptive leadership: Tools and tactics for changing your organization and the world*. Boston: Harvard Business School Publishing.

Hollis, J. (2018). *Living an examined life: Wisdom for the second half of the journey*. Boulder, CO: Sounds True, Inc.

Horney, K. (1945). *Our inner conflicts*. New York: W.W. Norton & Company.

Hudson, F.M. (1991). The adult years: Mastering the art of self renewal. San Francisco: Jossey-Bass.

Hudson, F.M. (1999). *The handbook of coaching: A comprehensive resource guide for managers, executives, consultants, and human resource professionals*. San Francisco: Jossey-Bass.

Iacoboni, M. (2009). Imitation, empathy, and mirror neurons. *Annual Review of Psychology, 60*, 653–670.

James, W. (1913). *The variety of religious experience*. London: Longmans, Green, and Co.

Kegan, R. (1982). *The evolving self*. Cambridge, MA: Harvard University Press.

Kets de Vries, M. (2014). *Mindful leadership coaching: Journeys into the interior*. Basingstoke, UK: Palgrave Macmillan.

Kline, N. (1999). *Time to think: Listening to ignite the human mind*. New York: Hachette Book Group.

Laske, O. (2006a). *Measuring hidden dimensions: The art and science of fully engaging adults*. Medford, MA: IDM Press.

Laske, O. (2006b). From coach training to coach education: Teaching coaching within a comprehensively evidence based framework. *International Journal of Evidence Based Coaching and Mentoring, 4*(1), 45–57.

Main, M., & Hesse, E. (1990). Parents' unresolved traumatic experiences are related to infant disorganized attachment status: Is frightened and/or frightening parental behavior the linking mechanism? In M. T. Greenberg, D. Cicchetti, & E. M. Cummings (Eds.), *Attachment in the preschool years* (pp. 161–182). Chicago: University of Chicago Press.

Main, M., & Solomon, J. (1986). Discovery of a new, insecure-disorganized/disoriented attachment pattern. In M. Yogman & T. B. Brazelton (Eds.), *Affective development in infancy* (pp. 95–124). Norwood, NJ: Ablex.

McLaren, K. (2010). *The language of emotions: What your feelings are trying to tell you.* Boulder, CO: Sounds True, Inc.

McLaren, K. (2013). *The art of empathy: A complete guide to life's most essential skill.* Boulder, CO: Sounds True, Inc.

McLean, P. (2012). *The completely revised handbook of coaching: A developmental approach.* San Francisco: Jossey-Bass.

Murdoch, E., & Patterson, E. (n.d.). Understanding what we mean by "WHO you are is HOW you COACH, SUPERVISE or WORK" [Abstract]. Coaching Supervision Academy. Retrieved from https://coachingsupervisionacademy.com/understanding-what-we-mean-by-who-you-are-is-how-you-coach-supervise-or-work-2/.

O'Neill, M.B. (2007). *Executive coaching with backbone and heart: A systems approach to engaging leaders with their challenges* (2nd ed.). San Francisco: Jossey-Bass.

Palmer, W. (2013). *Leadership embodiment: How the way we sit and stand can change the way we think and speak.* San Rafael, CA: The Embodiment Foundation.

Petrie, N. (2015). *The how-to of vertical leadership development – Part 2: 30 experts, 3 conditions, and 15 approaches* [White Paper]. Center for Creative Leadership. Retrieved from https://www.ccl.org/wp-content/uploads/2015/04/verticalLeadersPart2.pdf.

Putnam, D. (2004). *Psychological courage.* Lanham, MD: University Press of America.

Richards, M.C. (1964). *Centering: In pottery, poetry and the person.* Hanover, NH: University Press of New England.

Scharmer, O., & Kaufer, K. (2013). *Leading from the emerging future: From ego-system to eco-system economies.* San Francisco: Berrett-Koehler.

Scharmer, O. (2018). *The essentials of theory U: Core principles and applications.* San Francisco: Berrett-Koehler.

Schein, E. (2013). *Humble inquiry: The gentle art of asking instead of telling.* San Francisco: Berrett-Koehler.

Schein, E. (2018). *Humble leadership: The power of relationships, openness, and trust.* San Francisco: Berrett-Koehler.

Schön, D. (1987). *Educating the reflective practitioner.* San Francisco: Jossey-Bass.

Senge, P.M. (2006). *The fifth discipline.* New York: Doubleday.

Short, R. (1998). *Learning in relationship.* Bellevue, WA: Learning in Action Technologies.

Silsbee, D. (2008). *Presence-based coaching: Cultivating self-generative leaders through mind, body, and heart.* San Francisco: Jossey-Bass.

Siminovitch, D.E. (2017). *A gestalt coaching primer: The path toward awareness IQ.* Toronto, ON: Gestalt Coaching Works, LLC.

Solnit, R. (2014). *The faraway nearby.* New York: Penguin Books.

Strozzi-Heckler, R. (2014). *The art of somatic coaching: Embodying skillful action, wisdom, and compassion.* Berkeley, CA: North Atlantic Books.

U.S. Army Heritage and Education Center (2018). Who first originated the term VUCA (Volatility, Uncertainty, Complexity and Ambiguity)? [USAHEC Ask Us a Question. The United States Army War College]. Retrieved from http://usawc.libanswers.com/faq/84869.

Wampold, B.E. (2001). *The great psychotherapy debate: Models, methods, and findings.* New York: Routledge.

Yalom, I. (2002). *The gift of therapy: An open letter to a new generation of therapists and their patients.* New York: HarperCollins.

ABOUT THE AUTHOR

Pamela McLean, PhD, is the CEO and cofounder of The Hudson Institute of Coaching, an organization providing a full suite of coaching services inside organizations and widely known as one of the leading coach training programs in the United States for over 30 years. McLean brings more than three decades of experience as a clinical and organizational psychologist, a master coach, coach supervisor, and leader and contributor in the field of coaching. She has worked with hundreds of leaders inside organizations helping to strategically develop a coaching culture at all levels.

McLean has written extensively and authored *The Completely Revised Handbook of Coaching* (2012) and *LifeForward: Charting the Journey Ahead.* (2015). She served on the editorial board of the *International Journal of Coaching in Organizations* (IJCO) and coedited an issue dedicated to a developmental perspective on organizational coaching. Pam served on Harvard's JFK Women's Leadership Board, the faculty of Saybrook University in San Francisco, California, and LikeMinded in San Francisco. She is a member of the American Psychological Association's Division 13, Consulting Psychology and a Fellow of The American Group Psychotherapy Association. She is a frequent key presenter on leadership coaching and the use of Self as Coach and going deeper to do our best work.

Pamela lives in the foothills of Santa Barbara, California, and when she isn't immersed in leadership coaching and coach supervision, she enjoys cooking, entertaining, traveling, birding, reading, and developing her skills in ceramics.

INDEX

Page numbers followed by *f* and *t* refer to figures and tables, respectively.